Maths workout
For homework and practice

Bob Hartman and Mark Patmore

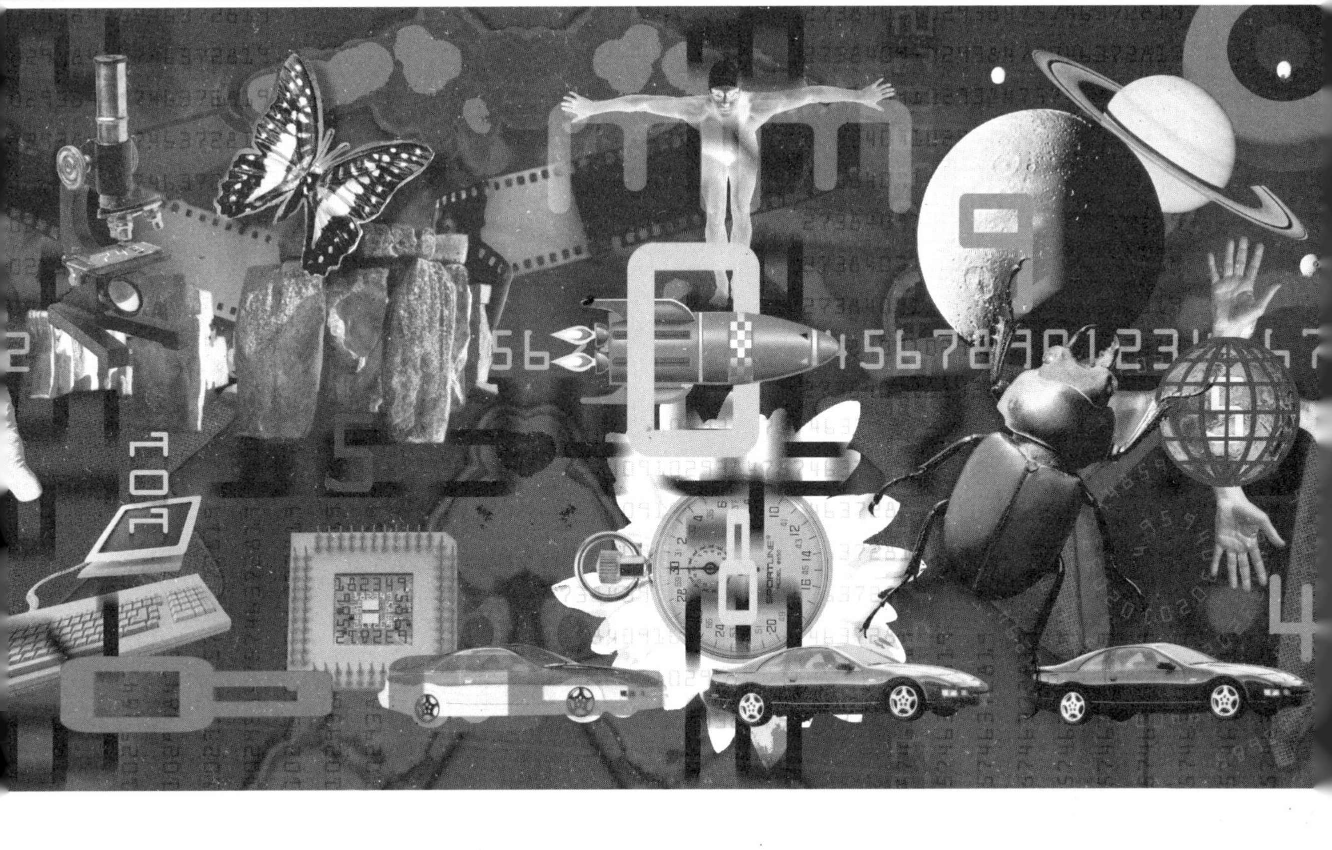

PUBLISHED BY THE PRESS SYNDICATE OF THE UNIVERSITY OF CAMBRIDGE
The Pitt Building, Trumpington Street, Cambridge, United Kingdom

CAMBRIDGE UNIVERSITY PRESS
The Edinburgh Building, Cambridge CB2 2RU, UK   http://www.cup.cam.ac.uk
40 West 20th Street, New York, NY 10011-4211, USA   http://www.cup.org
10 Stamford Road, Oakleigh, Melbourne 3166, Australia
Ruiz de Alarcón 13, 28014 Madrid, Spain

© Cambridge University Press 2000

First published 2000

Printed in the United Kingdom at the University Press, Cambridge

Produced by Gecko Limited, Bicester, Oxon

Typeface Stone serif 11/15.5pt   *System* QuarkXPress®

A catalogue record for this book is available from the British Library

ISBN 0 521 63486 5 paperback

NOTICE TO TEACHERS
It is illegal to reproduce any part of this work in material form (including photocopying and electronic storage) except under the following circumstances:
(i) where you are abiding by a licence granted to your school or institution by the Copyright Licensing Agency;
(ii) where no such licence exists, or where you wish to exceed the terms of a licence, and you have gained the written permission of Cambridge University Press;
(iii) where you are allowed to reproduce without permission under the provisions of Chapter 3 of the Copyright, Designs and Patents Act 1988.

Contents

1	Algebra practice 1	5
2	Algebra practice 2	7
3	Probability 1	10
4	Probability 2	13
5	Probability 3	16
6	Without a calculator 1	19
7	Without a calculator 2	22
8	Drawing and measuring	24
9	Solving equations	27
10	Solving problems with algebra	30
11	Inequalities	34
12	Decimal practice	38
13	Multiplication with decimals	41
14	Division with decimals	44
15	In your head 1	47
16	In your head 2	48

Extensions

1	Algebra practice 1	49
2	Algebra practice 2	50
3	Probability 1	51
4	Probability 2	51
5	Probability 3	53
8	Drawing and measuring	54
9	Solving equations	55
10	Solving problems with algebra	55
11	Inequalities	56
12	Decimal practice	58
13	Multiplication with decimals	59
14	Division with decimals	60
	Word list and definitions	61

Introduction

This book is intended for you to work through at home or at school, either on your own or with another person. It can be helpful to work with someone else and, as you will see, some questions do suggest that you will need to do this. Sharing ideas and knowledge and, above all, having to talk through what you are doing will help you to understand the work better and remember it more clearly.

There are 16 units in this book. Most units begin with a section called 'Key ideas'. This section is intended to remind you of the basic facts and skills you should have in order to answer the questions which follow. In all the units, except the mental mathematics units which are called 'In your head', there are three sets of questions labelled 'A', 'B' and 'C' which provide a range of questions, challenges, and activities for you to try. The A questions are straightforward and intended to ensure that you are confident with the basic concepts for the topic; the B and C questions are more challenging. The 'In your head' units have questions of equal difficulty but labelled 'A' and 'B' and for convenience.

Most units also have a set of 3 or 4 extension questions at the end of the book, and these are intended to challenge your knowledge and understanding further.

Sometimes you will need special equipment to complete the tasks. Wherever possible, we have intended you to use equipment that you should be able to find at home.

1 Algebra practice 1

A1 Write down expressions for the perimeters of these shapes.
All the lengths are in metres.

(a)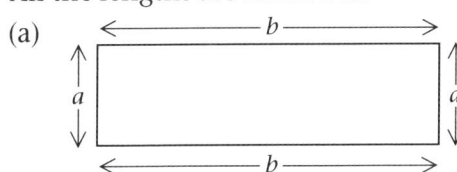

(b)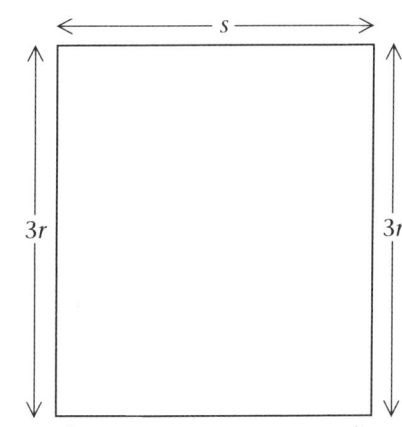

A2 Simplify these expressions.

(a) $x + x + x + x$

(b) $3 + c + 4$

(c) $2y + y$ (d) $4y - y$ (e) $y + y + y + y - y$

A3 When $x = 12$, $y = 3$, $z = 4$ find the value of:

(a) $x + y$ (b) xy (c) $x - y$ (d) $x + yz$

(e) $\frac{x}{y}$ (f) $2x + y$ (g) $2xz$ (h) $x + y + z$

B1 Simplify these expressions.
If it is not possible to simplify the expression, write down 'cannot be simplified'.

(a) $2x + 3x$ (b) $a + 2 + 4a$ (c) $3 + c + 2$ (d) $3d + c + d + c$

(e) $n + n + 3n$ (f) $d + 2c + d - c$ (g) $6x + 4y$ (h) $2a + b + 3a + 4b + 1$

B2 Write down expressions for the lengths marked with ?.
All the lengths are in metres.

(a)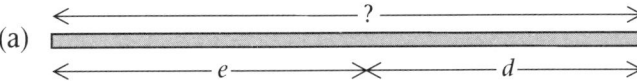

(b)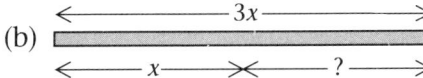

B3 The letter *n* represents a number. Write down expressions for the following.
  (a) twice the number
  (b) one more than the number
  (c) one less than the number
  (d) the number multiplied by 10
  (e) the number divided by 5
  (f) five divided by the number

C1 The power rating of a piece of electrical equipment is measured in watts.
It is calculated from the formula $P = VI$, where
  P is the power in watts,
  V is the voltage rating of the piece of equipment,
and I is the current in amps. Use the formula to answer these.
  (a) Find P when $V = 220$ volts and $I = 10$ amps.
  (b) When $V = 220$ volts and $P = 880$ watts, what is I?
  (c) Find the power ratings of some electrical devices at home.
  The voltage in most homes and schools is 220 volts.

C2 Here is part of a spreadsheet showing some of the formulas.
Work out the values of the numbers in the shaded cells.

	A	B	C	D
1	1	1	=A1 * B1	=A1 + B1 + C1
2	=A1 + 1	=B1 + 3	=A2 * B2	=A2 + B2 + C2
3	=A2 + 1	=B2 + 3	=A3 * B3	=A3 + B3 + C3
4	=A3 + 1	=B3 + 3	40	=A4 + B4 + C4
5	5	13	65	=A5 + B5 + C5
6	6	16	96	118
7	7	19	133	159
8	8	22	176	206

C3 All these shapes are made from rectangles measuring *x* by 3*x*.
(All measurements are in centimetres.)
Write down the perimeter of each of the shapes. What do you notice?

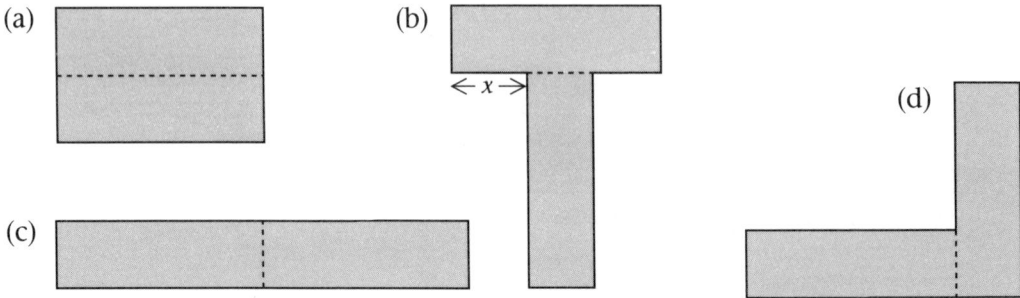

(a)   (b)   (d)
(c)

Experiment with some different-sized pairs of rectangles.

2 Algebra practice 2

A1 Copy and complete these.
(a) $2(x + 2y) = \;\square x + \square y$
(b) $\square(m + n) = 4m + 4n$
(c) $\square(5g + 4h) = 15g + 12h$
(d) $\square(2x + \square y) = 4x + 10y$

A2 Calculate the values of these expressions when $x = 4$, $y = 5$ and $z = 8$.
(a) $xy - z$
(b) $2x + yz$
(c) x^2
(d) $x^2 + y^2$
(e) $2x^2 + 1$
(f) x^2y^2

A3 Simplify these expressions as much as possible.
(a) $2xy + 3x + xy + x^2$
(b) $2x^2 + xy + y^2 + xy + 3x^2$
(c) $k + j + 2(k + 2j) + j(j + k)$
(d) $a + b + c + ab + 2bc + 2ca + ac$

A4 Find the values of x which make these expressions true.
(a) $2x + 1 = 11$
(b) $4x = 2$
(c) $4x = 1$
(d) $x^2 = 16$
(e) $x \div 3 = 4$
(f) $2(x + 1) = 10$

B1 Write these as simply as possible.
(a) $2p + 5q + p + 3q$
(b) $4 \times 3x + 6x$
(c) $4s \times 2t \times 3u$
(d) $12xy \div 4$

B2 Substitute $m = 4$ and $n = 2$ to find the values of:
(a) $7mn$
(b) $m \div n$
(c) $n \div m$
(d) $m^2 - n^2$
(e) $3m^2 - 10n$
(f) $m(2n + 1)$.

B3 A, B, C and D are points on a straight line.

Use x, y and z to write expressions for these lengths.
(a) AD
(b) BC
(c) CD
(d) The distance from A of the point half-way along AD.

7

B4 Here is the output from a spreadsheet. Which one(s) – if any – of the sets of formulas shown below could have produced this output?

	A	B	C	D
1	1	2	1	4
2	2	4	3	9
3	3	6	5	14
4	4	8	7	19

Workbook 1

(a)

	A	B	C	D
1	= 1	2	= 4 * A1 – 3	= 5 * A1 – 4
2	= 2 * A1 – 1	= B1 + 2	= 4 * A2 – 3	= 5 * A2 – 4
3	= 2 * A2 – 1	= B2 + 2	= 4 * A3 – 3	= 5 * A3 – 4
4	= 2 * A3 – 1	= B3 + 2	= 4 * A4 – 3	= 5 * A4 – 4

(b)

	A	B	C	D
1	= 1	= 2 * A1	= 1	= 5 * A1 – 1
2	= A1 + 1	= 2 * A2	= C1 + 2	= 5 * A2 – 1
3	= A2 + 1	= 2 * A3	= C2 + 2	= 5 * A3 – 1
4	= A3 + 1	= 2 * A4	= C3 + 2	= 5 * A4 – 1

(c)

	A	B	C	D
1	= 1	= 2 * A1	= B1 –1	= (3 * B1 + 2 * C1)/2
2	= A1 + 1	= 2 * A2	= B2 – 1	= (3 * B2 + 2 * C1)/2
3	= A2 + 1	= 2 * A3	= B3 – 1	= (3 * B3 + 2 * C1)/2
4	= A3 + 1	= 2 * A4	= B4 – 1	= (3 * B4 + 2 * C1)/2

(d)

	A	B	C	D
1	= 1	= 2 * A1	= 2 * A1 – 1	= 3 * A1 + C1
2	= A1 + 1	= 2 * A2	= 2 * A2 – 1	= 3 * A2 + C2
3	= A2 + 1	= 2 * A3	= 2 * A3 – 1	= 3 * A3 + C3
4	= A3 + 1	= 2 * A4	= 2 * A4 – 1	= 3 * A4 + C4

(e)

	A	B	C	D
1	= 1	= 2	= 1	= 4
2	= A1 + 1	= B1 + 2	= C1 + 2	= D1 + 5
3	= A2 + 1	= B2 + 2	= C2 + 2	= D2 + 5
4	= A3 + 1	= B3 + 2	= C3 + 2	= D3 + 5

(f)

	A	B	C	D
1	= 1	= 2	= 2 * B1 – 3	= 4 * A1
2	= A1 + 1	= 2 * A2	= B2 – 1	= 4 * A2
3	= A2 + 1	= 2 * A3	= B3 – 1	= 4 * A3
4	= A3 + 1	= 2 * A4	= B4 – 1	= 4 * A4

(g)

	A	B	C	D
1	= 1	= 2 * A1	= 2 * A1 – 1	= A1 + B1 + C1
2	= A1 + 1	= 2 * A2	= 2 * A2 – 1	= A2 + B2 + C2
3	= A2 + 1	= 2 * A3	= 2 * A3 – 1	= A3 + B3 + C3
4	= A3 + 1	= 2 * A4	= 2 * A4 – 1	= A4 + B4 + C4

(h)

	A	B	C	D
1	= 1	2	= 4 * A1 – 3	= 5 * A1 – 4
2	= A1 + 1	= B1 * 2	= 4 * A2 – 3	= 5 * A2 – 4
3	= A2 + 1	= B2 * 2	= 4 * A3 – 3	= 5 * A3 – 4
4	= A3 + 1	= B3 * 2	= 4 * A4 – 3	= 5 * A4 – 4

8

C1 Computer games rely on the game rules being put into mathematical statements. For example, imagine a game played with a red 1–6 dice and a black 1–6 dice, where

> r is the number on the red dice
> b is the number on the black dice.

Winning outcomes could be $r + b = 7$ or $2r + b = 10$.
(So *if $r + b = 7$ or $2r + b = 10$ then* you win.)

(a) Make a table showing all the possible winning throws for the winning rule $r + b = 7$.

(b) In a lot of games you need a 'double' to start.
Write this winning rule as a mathematical statement.

(c) In a particular game the product of the numbers on each dice must be 6 for a win. Write this as a mathematical statement.
List all the different ways in which you could win with this rule.

 Challenge Look for the rules of some dice games – try to write some of these as mathematical statements.

C2 (a) Show that this 3 by 3 grid forms an algebraic magic square.

(b) What is special about the magic squares formed when:
   i) $m = 9$, $a = 6$, $b = 2$
   ii) $m = 37$, $a = 30$, $b = 6$?

$m+a$	$m-a-b$	$m+b$
$m-a+b$	m	$m+a-b$
$m-b$	$m+a+b$	$m-a$

C3 (a) Write down in words the rule connecting the numbers in the circles with the numbers in the rectangles in this triangular arithmagon.

(b) Write down the rule connecting the sum of the numbers in the circles with the sum of the numbers in the rectangles.

(c) Investigate square- or pentagon-shaped arithmagons.

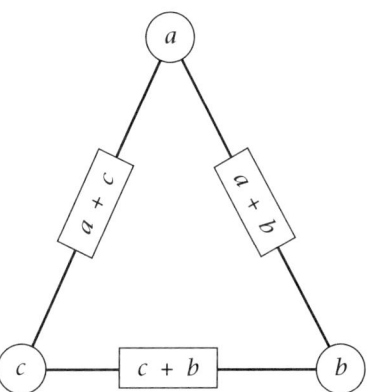

3 Probability 1

Key ideas

The probability or chance of an event occurring is measured on a scale of 0 to 1.
   An event that is certain to happen has a probability of 1 (or 100%).
   An event with can't possibly occur has a probability of zero (or 0%).

The probability of an event happening in a situation can be calculated if:
• all the outcomes that can occur in the situation can be counted,
• all these outcomes are equally likely.

The formula to use is:

$$\text{Probability of an event} = \frac{\text{number of ways that the event can be an outcome}}{\text{total number of different outcomes}}$$

So the probability of throwing a square number with a fair 6-sided dice is

$$= \frac{\text{number of ways to throw a square number}}{\text{total number of different outcomes when a dice is thrown}}$$

$$= \frac{\text{there are two ways to throw a square number (a 1 or a 4)}}{\text{number of different outcomes when a dice is thrown (1, 2, 3, 4, 5 or 6)}}$$

$$= \frac{2}{6} \text{ or } \frac{1}{3}$$ (We don't usually simplify fractions in probability unless asked to.)

It is important not to forget that all the *outcomes must be equally likely*, in order to use the formula. For example,

'What's the probability of the Little Brock team beating Brazil at football?'

There are three possible outcomes for the Little Brock team: win, lose or draw, but the probability of Little Brock winning *is not* $\frac{1}{3}$ because win, lose or draw are not equally likely.

A1 When a normal 6-sided dice is thrown, how many ways can each of these events be an outcome:

(a) a score of 3   (b) a score of 6   (c) a score of 7

(d) a score of 1 or 2   (e) a score between 1 and 6   (f) an even score?

A2 Write down the probability of each of the events in question A1.

A3 When a dice is thrown, what is the probability of getting a number bigger than 3?

A4 What is the probability, when tossing a fair coin, of getting a tail?

> ### Key ideas
>
> The word **random** is often used in probability problems. For example, 'a car in a car park is **chosen at random**'. It means that each car had an equal chance, or was equally likely, to be chosen. Another phrase is '**without looking**', for example, 'a chocolate is chosen without looking'.
> This means that each chocolate is equally likely to be picked.
>
> If the probability of an event happening is p,
> then the probability of it *not* happening is $1 - p$.
>
> The probability of throwing 1 with a 6-sided dice is $\frac{1}{6}$,
> so the probability of *not* throwing a 1 is $1 - \frac{1}{6} = \frac{5}{6}$.

B1 There are 5 blue and 4 red counters in a bag.

A counter is taken at random. What is the probability that this counter is:

(a) blue (b) red (c) not red (d) black?

B2 When an 8-sided dice, with faces numbered 1 to 8, is thrown, what is the probability that it will show:

(a) an odd number (b) a prime number (c) a number greater than 4

(d) a number not greater than 4 (e) a 6 or 5 (f) an odd prime number

(g) not an odd prime number (h) a number less than 3?

B3 There are twelve cars in a small car park. These are:

Red Toyota	Black Ford	Red Ford	Blue Toyota
White Vauxhall	Red Toyota	Black Ford	Red Ford
Blue Ford	White Toyota	Red Toyota	Green Ford.

(a) How many of the cars in the car park are: i) Fords ii) Toyotas?

(b) A car thief tries to break into one of the cars. He chooses this car at random. What is the probability that the car is: i) a Ford ii) a Toyota?

(c) What is the probability that the thief tries to steal

 i) a red car ii) not a red car iii) a green Toyota?

B4 The letters from the word PROBABILITY are written on to pieces of paper.
One of these pieces of paper is taken at random without looking.
What is the probability that the letter is:

(a) 'P'   (b) 'B'   (c) not a 'B'   (d) 'A' or 'B'   (e) 'Z'?

C1 Seven letters arrive at the Smiths' house.
The Smiths' first names are James and Jennifer.
All the letters are addressed to J. Smith.
Three of the letters are for James. The others are for Jennifer.

(a) What is the probability that the first letter opened is for Jennifer?

(b) What is the probability that the first letter opened is for James?

C2 A combination lock on a brief case has three rings, each with the digits 0 to 9 on it.

(a) What is the smallest number made by the digits on the lock?

(b) What is the largest number made by the digits on the lock?

(c) How many different 3-digit numbers can be made with the digits on the lock?

(d) What is the probability, if you don't know the combination, of finding the correct combination by chance on the first try?

C3 These dominoes are placed face down on the table.

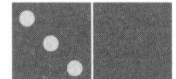 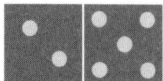  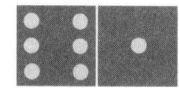 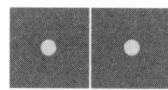

Without looking, Rajit picks up one of the dominoes.
What is the probability that Rajit will pick up a domino with

(a) a six on it   (b) a blank on it   (c) a three on it

(d) a total of 7 spots   (e) a total of more than one spot?

C4 A box of chocolates contains: 7 plain chocolates, 5 milk chocolates and 3 white chocolates. Rik takes a chocolate at random.
What is the probability that it is:

(a) a plain chocolate   (b) a milk or white chocolate

(c) not a milk or white chocolate?

4 Probability 2

Key ideas

For **equally likely outcomes** this equation can be used to calculate the **theoretical probability** of an event.

$$\text{Probability of an event} = \frac{\text{number of ways that the event can be an outcome}}{\text{total number of different outcomes}}$$

This means that most theoretical probability questions involve counting or listing numbers of outcomes.

Listing outcomes is helped if you are **systematic**. For example, when listing all the three-letter **combinations** of A, B and C, if you begin in a haphazard way such as: CBA   BCA   CAB   …   there is a good chance of missing out or repeating a combination. One way to be systematic is to begin like this:
ABC   ACB   BCA   BAC   …

When names or labels are involved, using initial letters can help. For example, a cafe sells baked potatoes. You can have 2 fillings from the choice of *c*heese, *t*una, *s*alad and *b*eans. How many different fillings are possible?
Using the initials gives: CT   CS   CB   …
Complete the list yourself. The answer is given upside down below.

When listing the different outcomes involving dice or coins remember that, for example, a head on the first coin and a tail on the second coin is a different outcome from a tail on the first coin and a head on the second coin.

There are a total of six different fillings: CT, CS, CB, TS, TB, SB

Don't forget, be systematic in your listing.

A1 Using H for heads and T for tails:

(a) list the four possible outcomes when two coins are tossed,

(b) list all the possible outcomes when three coins are tossed,

(c) use your answers to calculate the probability of getting all heads when i) two coins and ii) three coins are tossed.

A2 List all the possible outcomes when a coin is tossed and a 6-sided dice is rolled.

A3 List all the 3-digit numbers which can be made from the digits 1, 2 and 3. The same digit can be used up to three times in each number.

A4 There are four teams in a relay race. They are called red, blue, green and yellow.
There are just two prizes, one for first and one for second.
List all the different ways that the two prizes can be won.

B1 This table shows all the possible results formed when any of the digits 1, 2, 3 or 4 are multiplied together.

(a) What is the total number of outcomes?

(b) How many of the outcomes give a result of:
  i) 16   ii) 3   iii) 4?

(c) Two digits in the range 1 to 4 are picked at random. (The same digit may be picked twice.) What is the probability that the product of these two digits is:
  i) 16   ii) 3   iii) 4   iv) even   v) greater than 5?

first digit

second digit

×	1	2	3	4
1	1	2	3	4
2	2	4	6	8
3	3	6	9	12
4	4	8	12	16

B2 Here is a sketch of a square table.
People may sit at any of the four positions A, B, C or D.

(a) List all the positions that two people can sit at.

(b) What is the probability that two people who choose where they sit at random, happen to end up facing each other?

B3 A teacher wants to design a game, using dice, to test students' divisions.
The game uses a normal 6-sided red dice and a normal 6-sided black dice.
The students have to divide the number on the black dice by the number on the red dice, but the teacher does not want too many divisions with answers that are recurring decimals, such as $0.\dot{3}$ or $1.\dot{6}$.
The teacher draws up a table showing all the possible divisions and answers.

(a) Copy and complete the teacher's table.

(b) Calculate the probability of getting a division with an answer that is a recurring decimal.

(c) Use your answer to (b) to decide if the game should use something other than dice.

Red dice

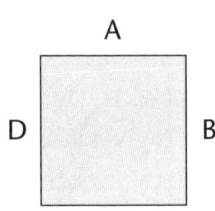

14

B4 In a breakfast cereal competition entrants have to list in winning order the 3 features of a new car.

Feature	
In-car sound system	1
Acceleration	2
Styling	3

(a) How many different orderings are there?

(b) What is the probability of winning the competition by making a random selection?

C1 Here is a question and a student's answer.
Read it through carefully.
Is the student correct? Explain your answer.

Q. Two coins are tossed, what is the probability of getting a Head and a Tail?

A. There is only one way of getting a Head and a Tail.

There is a total of three different outcomes. These are HH, TT and HT.

Therefore the probability of getting a Head and a Tail is $\frac{1}{3}$.

C2 This diagram shows the battery chamber of a calculator.

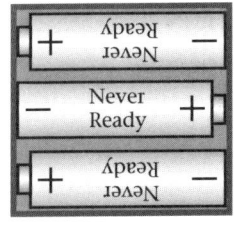

It holds 3 batteries.

Each battery can fit in place in two possible ways.

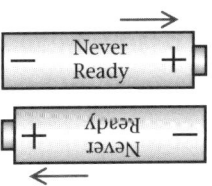

(a) How many different ways can the batteries be fitted?

(b) These are the only two correct ways of connecting the three batteries.
What is the probability of connecting the batteries in the correct way by chance?

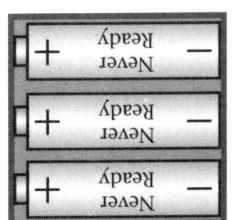 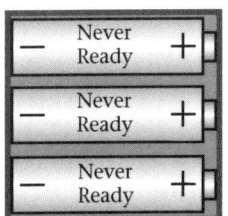

C3 (a) What is the probability, when three coins are tossed, that the result is 2 Heads and 1 Tail?

(b) What is the probability that the result is 2 Tails and 1 Head?

(c) What is the probability of *not* getting all 3 coins the same?

15

5 Probability 3

Key ideas

Here is a table showing the results of throwing two dice 89 times and recording the difference between the two scores each time.

Difference	Tally	Frequency
0	卌 卌 ||||	14
1	卌 卌 卌 卌 卌 |	26
2	卌 卌 卌 卌 |	21
3	卌 卌 卌	15
4	卌 ||||	9
5	||||	4
	Total =	89

The **frequency of an event** is the number of times it occurs.
For the results shown here the frequency of 'a difference of 1' is 26 – 'a difference of 1' occurred 26 times.

The **relative frequency of an event** is the proportion of times it occurs.
In all there are 89 results here, of which 26 resulted in 'a difference of 1', so the relative frequency of 'a difference of 1' is $\frac{26}{89}$.

The relative frequency of an event gives the **estimated** or **experimental probability** that it will occur.

The estimated (experimental) probability of 'a difference of 1' is therefore $\frac{26}{89}$.

You will need some 6-sided dice for some of these questions.

A1 Here is a table showing the results of throwing two 6-sided dice and recording the larger score.
(If the two scores are the same use this number.)
Use the table to answer these.

Larger score	Tally	Frequency
1	卌 |	6
2	卌 卌 卌 ||	17
3	卌 卌 卌 卌 卌 |||	28
4	卌 卌 卌 卌 卌 卌 卌 ||||	39
5	卌 卌 卌 卌 卌 卌 卌 卌 卌 |||	48
6	卌 卌 卌 卌 卌 卌 卌 卌 卌 卌 卌 卌 |	61

(a) What is the total number of results?

(b) What is the most likely larger score?

(c) What is the probability of getting a larger score of 3?

(d) What is the probability of getting a larger score of 6?

A2 If you were to repeat the experiment in A1 would you expect to get exactly the same results? Give reasons for your answer.

Now repeat the experiment and use your results to answer parts (a) – (d) in A1.

It will speed things up if you work with a partner.

A3 This table shows the larger score when two dice are thrown.

Use the table to answer these questions.

(a) What is the most likely larger score?

(b) Write down the 'larger scores' in order of their probability of occurring.

First dice \ Second dice	1	2	3	4	5	6
1	1	2	3	4	5	6
2	2	2	3	4	5	6
3	3	3	3	4	5	6
4	4	4	4	4	5	6
5	5	5	5	5	5	6
6	6	6	6	6	6	6

A4 (a) Copy and complete this table which shows the difference in the two scores when two dice are thrown.

(b) What is the most likely difference in scores?

(c) Write down the 'differences in scores' in order of their probability.

(d) Your answers to (c) involve **theoretical probabilities**.
How do they compare with those calculated from the experimental probabilities using the data shown in the table in the *Key ideas*?

First dice \ Second dice	1	2	3	4	5	6
1	0	1	2	3	4	
2	1	0				
3	2					
4	3					
5	4					
6						

B1 This table shows how many sixes there were when twelve dice were thrown 100 times.

Number of sixes	0	1	2	3	4	5	6
Frequency	14	28	26	19	9	3	1

(a) How many 6s are most likely to come up when 12 dice are thrown?

(b) What is the experimental probability of getting no 6s?

(c) What is the experimental probability of getting four or more 6s?

(d) If you threw a set of twelve dice 50 times, about how many times would you expect there to be no sixes?

B2 Here are the results showing the total score when two dice are thrown.

```
5  8  11  5   2   6   8  2  6  9  8  7
5  4  5   7   11  6   5  3  6  6  9  3
2  6  9   6   10  3   5  3  7  8  5  5
3  2  11  9   11  5   10 7  5  6  8  8
6  3  8   5   2   12  9  3  7  9  3  9
```

Use this data to find the experimental probability that the total score with two dice will divide by   (a) 3   (b) 4   (c) 5.

B3 Find the experimental probability of at least 1 double when four dice are thrown. Think carefully about how many times you will need to repeat the experiment.

Key ideas

Sometimes fractions have to be compared. For example, is $\frac{5}{12}$ greater than $\frac{7}{19}$?

One way is to convert each fraction to a decimal: $\frac{5}{12} = 5 \div 12$ and $\frac{7}{19} = 7 \div 19 \ldots$

C1 Look back at question B2. Work out the theoretical probability for parts (a) to (c). Would you expect the sets of answers to be the same? Try to explain your answer.

C2 Find the probability that when three dice are thrown, all three dice show a different score. Write a brief account of what you did – show it to a friend to see if they understand (and agree with) your conclusions.

C3 Investigate this statement for yourself: 'When three dice are thrown, the middle score has a 50% probability of being 4 or above.'

6 Without a calculator 1

Do not use a calculator for this unit.
You may need to do a little revision – the word list on pages 61–63 might be useful for this.

A1 What is the sum of the first 5 square numbers?

A2 A line of length 4 metres is divided into 5 equal parts.
What is the length of one of these parts?

A3 On average there are 385 words on each page of a book.
The book has 64 pages. How many words does it contain?

A4 The fifth triangle number is $\frac{5 \times 6}{2} = 15$.

The sixth triangle number is $\frac{6 \times 7}{2} = 21$.

The seventh triangle number is $\frac{7 \times 8}{2} = 28$.

What is the (a) third (b) twelfth (c) fiftieth (d) nth triangle number?

A5 What is the mean of:
(a) 2 3 4 5 6   (b) 122 123 124 125 126?

(c) Look at your answers to (a) and (b). Describe a quick way to find,
for example, the mean of the numbers: 574 575 576 577 578.

A6 Calculate the perimeter of this shape.

A7 Which of the numbers below is prime?
Show how you went about finding
which one is prime.

(a) 221   (b) 212   (c) 211   (d) 121

A8 Find the mean of $\frac{1}{2}$ $1\frac{1}{2}$ $2\frac{1}{4}$ 2 $2\frac{3}{4}$.

A9 Find the median number in this list of numbers.

73 79 78 76 77 79 80 79 74 72 76

A10 Estimate the answers to these calculations.
Show clearly how you arrived at your answers.

(a) $183 \div 6.1$ (b) 901×37 (c) $19.7 \div 4.7$ (d) $\frac{2.87 \times 11.6}{3.91}$

B1 (a) Arrange these temperatures in order. Start with the lowest temperature.

7°C ⁻3°C 6°C ⁻5°C ⁻10°C 10°C 2°C

(b) Calculate the mean temperature.

B2 Is this mathematical statement: 1048 ÷ 8 = (1000 ÷ 8) + (48 ÷ 8) correct?

What about the mathematical statement: 2015 ÷ 9 = (2000 ÷ 9) + (15 ÷ 9)?

Show figures to support your answers.

B3 Calculating differences is a useful method to use when investigating sequences. For example, here are the 1st, 2nd and 3rd differences for the sequence of pentagon numbers   1   5   12   22   35   ...

pentagon numbers	1	5	12	22	35
first difference		4	7	10	13
second difference			3	3	3
third difference				0	0

(a) Use the pattern in differences to write down the next two pentagon numbers.

(b) Use differences to find the next two numbers in this sequence.

1   6   15   28   45   66

B4 What is the sum of the first six prime numbers?

B5 Find the missing digits in these calculations.

(a) ◯2◯ × 7 = 1◯7◯   (b) 3◯ − ◯9 = 9

B6 Many numbers can be written as the difference of two square numbers, for example, 5 = 9 − 4 (= $3^2 − 2^2$) and 20 = 36 − 16 (= $6^2 − 4^2$).

Which numbers under 20 cannot be written as the difference of two squares?

Try to find a pattern in these numbers.

B7 Find two consecutive whole numbers whose squares differ by 13.

B8 James gets paid £6.24 an hour. How much will he be paid for working $36\frac{1}{2}$ hours?

B9 Write the fractions (a) $\frac{2973}{14865}$ and (b) $\frac{3942}{15768}$ in their simplest terms.

B10 How many $4\frac{1}{2}$ cm lengths of wire can be cut from a 90 cm length of wire?

C1 In these calculations each letter represents a digit.

(a) What do the other letters represent if E represents 1 and U represents 9?

(There may be more than one solution.)
```
   THREE
   THREE
   F OUR
   -----
   ELEVEN
```

(b) What do A, B and C represent here?
$$BC \times BC = ABC$$

(c) What do A, B and C represent here?
$$ABC \div BB = B$$

C2 The date 14 July 1998 may be written 14/7/98.
It is an interesting date because $14 \times 7 = 98$.
Try to find some other dates where the product of the day and month gives the year (minus the century).

C3 Here are three examples of consecutive odd numbers:

    3, 5   17, 19, 21   11, 13, 15

Investigate the sums of (a) two (b) three and (c) four consecutive odd numbers. Try to summarise your findings.

C4 Draw a square.
Put any four numbers at the corners.
At the middle of each side write down the difference between the two corner numbers.

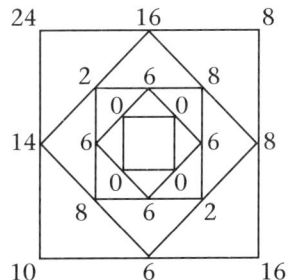

Join up these 4 points to make another square.
Repeat the instructions above.

Do you always end up with five squares? Do you always end up with zeros? Investigate.

C5 Continue this calculation pattern.
Find a pattern in the remainders.

$2519 \div 10 =$
$2519 \div 9 =$
$2519 \div 8 =$
$2519 \div 7 =$
…   …   …

7 Without a calculator 2

Do not use a calculator for this unit.
You may need to do a little revision – the word list on pages 61–63 might be useful for this.

A1 The sequence of triangle numbers is:

    1   3   6   10   15   21.

(a) Continue the sequence. Do any triangle numbers end in 2, 4, 7 or 9?

(b) Over two thousand years ago the ancient Greeks found a connection between triangle numbers (represented by T) and square numbers (S). It is $8T + 1 = S$. Test this formula with some examples of your own.

A2 Choose any three different digits.
Write down all the six possible 2-digit numbers using your three digits.
Find the sum of these six numbers.
Divide the result by the sum of the original three digits.
What do you notice?
Investigate for other sets of three starting digits.

A3 Choose some prime numbers to investigate the following.

(a) Square a prime number greater than 3. Add 14 to the result. What is the remainder when this is divided by 12?

(b) Square a prime number greater than 3. Add 12 to the result. What is the remainder when this is divided by 12?

A4 Work out the product of 1089 and 9. What do you notice?

A5 In the mathematical statement '6 × 3 = 2' the digits are correct but they are in incorrect positions. The correct statement is 3 × 2 = 6 (or 2 × 3 = 6).
In these calculations all the digits are correct, but they are in the wrong places. Write the correct mathematical statements – there may be more than one.

(a) 14 × 82 = 2   (b) 18 + 38 = 20   (c) 82 − 36 = 21

B1 Complete this pattern of calculations and their answers.
What do you notice?

    143 × 2 × 7 = 2002
    143 × 3 × 7 = …
    143 × 4 × 7 = …
    143 × 5 × 7 = …
    …   …   …   …

B2 In the case of the numbers 120 and 20, the first number is 6 times the second. Which number (the same one in each case) must be added to each so that in the resulting two numbers, the first number is three times the second? What about two times the second, or five times the second? Investigate.

B3 Try to solve this ancient Chinese puzzle.
It was invented over 2000 years ago.
'There is a cage containing rabbits and pheasants. In all there are 35 heads and 94 feet. How many of each animal are there in the cage?'

B4 Find the smallest number which will divide exactly by all of the 9 digits.

B5 There are three numbers.
Taken two at a time they add up to 15, 19 and 22.
What are the three numbers?

C1 Choose any whole number between 1 and 12, add 9 to it and double your answer. Now subtract the original number. Add together the digits of your final answer. What do you notice? Investigate for other starting numbers.

C2 When you multiply any number ending in 5 by another number ending in 5 the answer also ends in 5. Try to find some more cases which have a similar property.

C3 (a) Find as many 4-digit numbers as you can, which use the digits 1, 2, 3 and 4 once each and which are multiples of

    i) 2   ii) 3   iii) 4   iv) 5.

Check your answers by doing the necessary divisions.

  (b) Jot down the simple tests which will tell, without actually doing the calculations, whether or not a number is divisible by 2, 3, 4 or 5.
How can you combine the tests to test for divisibility by

    i) 6   ii) 12   iii) 15?

  (c) Jot down all the 5-digit numbers, if any, made from using 1, 2, 3, 4 and 5 once each which are multiples of

    i) 4   ii) 12   iii) 15.

Check your answers by doing the necessary divisions.

8 Drawing and measuring

Key ideas

Bisect means to cut into two equal parts.
The line XY bisects the line AB.
We say that XY is the bisector of AB, AP = PB.

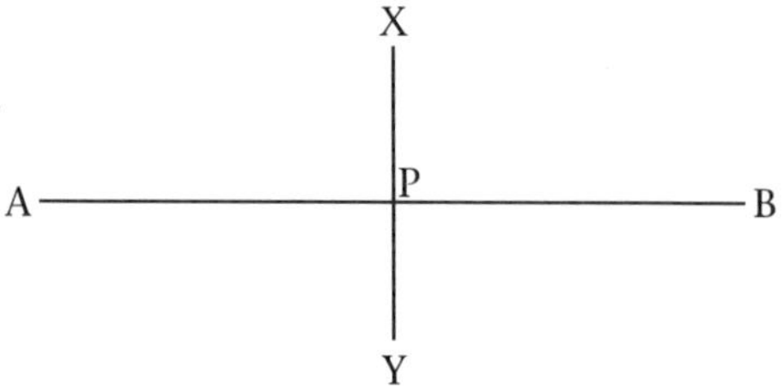

In the same way we say that
MR is the bisector of angle LMN,
or ∠LMN, so ∠LMR = ∠RMN.
Check that this is true using
a protractor or other
angle measurer.

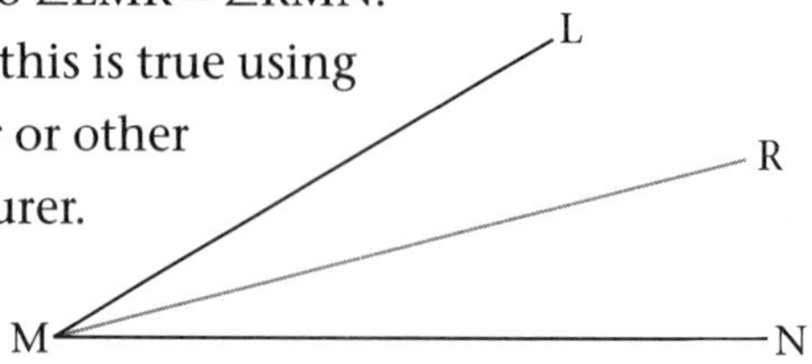

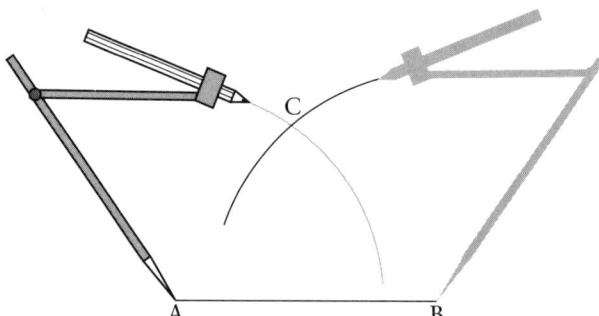

You need to be able to use compasses to draw a circle of any given radius.

Compasses can be used to construct triangles with sides of given length.

The line AB is 4cm long.

Every point on the grey arc is 2.5cm from A.

Everywhere on the black arc is 3cm from B.

So for the triangle ABC: AB = 4cm, BC = 3cm and CA = 2.5cm.

These two figures are **congruent**.
They are identical in shape and size.
The pairs of corresponding sides and angles
are equal. If you cut the figures out,
you could fit one exactly on top of the other.

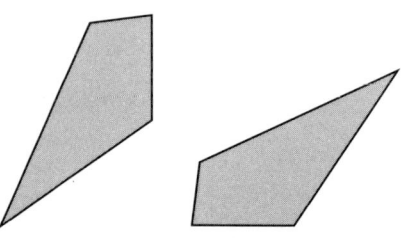

You will need a ruler, an angle measurer or protractor, squared paper, compasses.

A1 Here are some shapes. There are some pairs of congruent shapes.
Find which shapes are congruent by measuring.

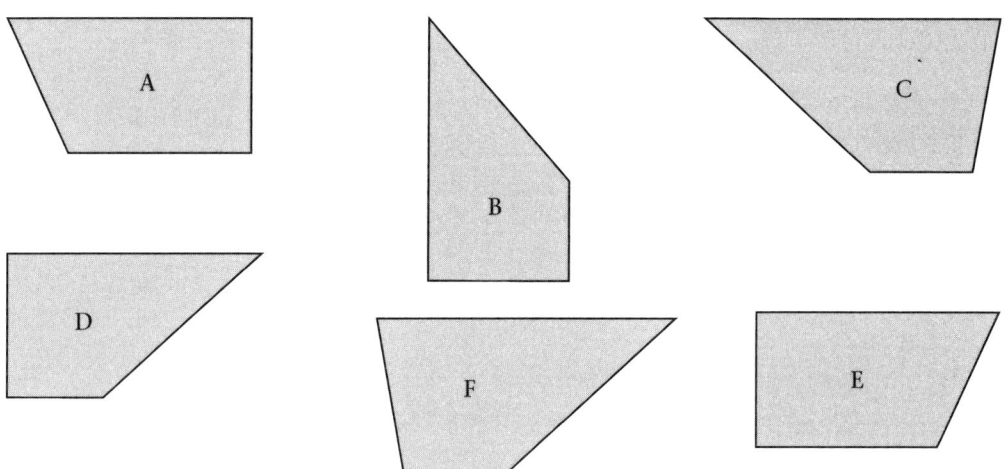

A2 On a piece of squared paper draw a grid with values of the *x*- and *y*-axes going from ⁻5 to 5. On the grid plot each of these points, which are the vertices (corners) of triangles. Find the perimeter of each triangle and write down what sort of triangle it is, for example, right-angled, isosceles, etc.

(a) A(1, 3) B(4, 1) C(1, 1) (b) D(⁻3, 1) E(⁻2, 5) F(⁻1, 1)

(c) G(⁻4, ⁻4) H(⁻3, ⁻2) I(⁻2, ⁻5) (d) J(2, ⁻4) K(4, ⁻2) L(4, ⁻4)

A3 By taking measurements and using a ruler and compasses only, make exact copies of these shapes.

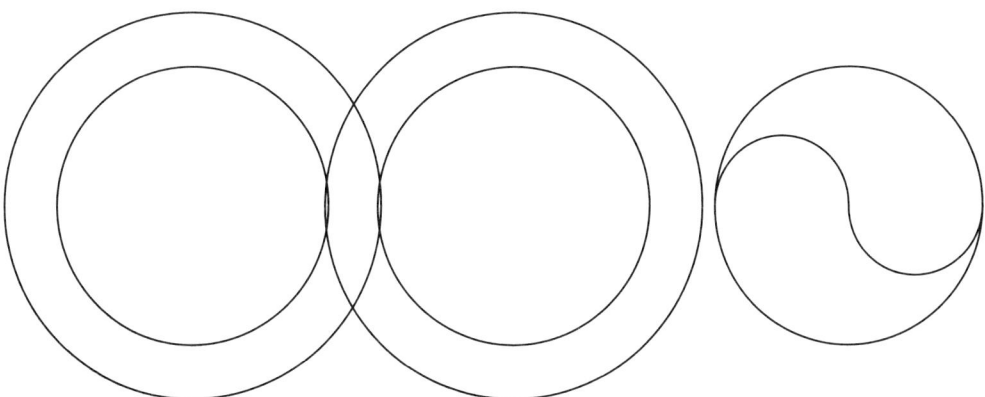

B1 Here are sketches of some shapes. Make accurate full-size drawings of them. Measure the other sides and angles as accurately as you can.

(a) (b) (c)

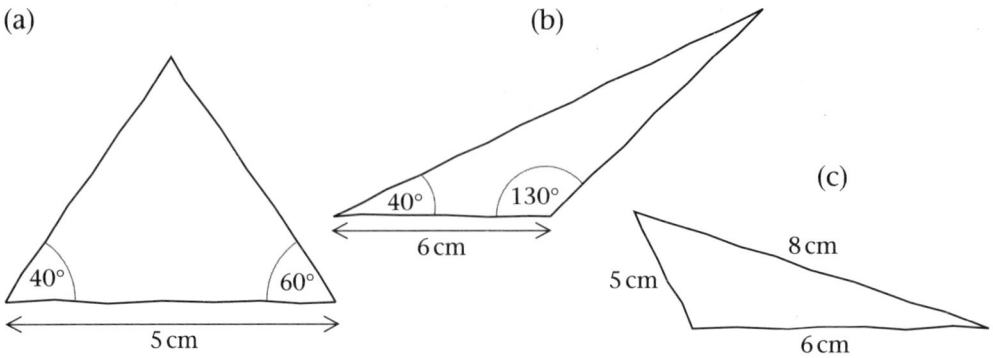

B2 Draw two spots 6 cm apart.
Label them A and B.
Find two points which are 5 cm from A *and also* 6 cm from B.
Check your answer by drawing and measuring.

B3 Zoe says that in any triangle the longest side is opposite the largest angle, and the shortest side is opposite the smallest angle. Investigate this for a few triangles of your own. Are there any cases where Zoe's 'rule' breaks down?

C1 Is it possible to construct triangles with sides of these lengths?

(a) 1 cm, 2 cm, 3 cm   (b) 2 cm, 4 cm, 6 cm

(c) 3 cm, 4 cm, 5 cm   (d) 1 cm, 2 cm, 4 cm

(e) Is there any way or rule which tells whether or not certain triangles are possible to draw?

C2 Draw a quadrilateral. Measure the angle of each corner and draw in the line which bisects it.
Do this for all the angles of the quadrilateral.
What shape do the four bisecting lines form?

not to scale

C3 Draw this pattern. Choose how big you want it to be.

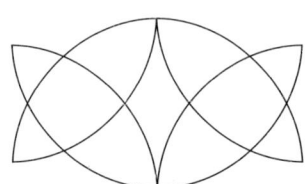

9 Solving equations

Key ideas

An **equation** is a mathematical statement containing an equals sign (=). It shows that two expressions (the left-hand side and the right-hand side) are equal. These are examples of equations.

$$2x = 14 \qquad 2a + 3 = 11 \qquad 3m + 1 = 2m + 7$$
$$8p + 3 = 6p + 15 \qquad \frac{x}{2} = 3 \qquad 2a = 1$$

Solving an equation means finding the unknown number, which is represented by a letter in the equation, that makes the mathematical statement true.

Whatever you do to one side you must do to the other side.
(Doing this ensures that the equation always 'balances'.)

For example, you can add or subtract the same quantity from each side or multiply or divide each side by the same quantity. Here is an example.

If $2x = 6 - x$

adding x to both sides: $\qquad 2x + x = 6 - x + x$
which gives $\qquad 3x = 6$
dividing each side by 3: $\qquad x = 2$ (the solution).

Always show each step in your working.
Check your solution by substituting back into the original equation.
If your solution is correct *the left-hand side will equal the right-hand side*.

Make sure you can solve the six equations above.
The solutions are given upside-down at the bottom of the page.

A1 Sometimes it is possible to solve equations just by looking at them.
This is called solving equations by **inspection**.
Try to solve these equations by inspection – just jot down the solutions.

(a) $x - 1 = 7$ (b) $x - 5 = 5$ (c) $z + 4 = 10$ (d) $p + 3 = 10$
(e) $20 + z = 23$ (f) $10p = 30$ (g) $4n = 16$ (h) $m + m + m = 12$

A2 Solve these equations by inspection. (Remember $\frac{x}{3}$ means '$x \div 3$'.)

(a) $\frac{x}{3} = 2$ (b) $\frac{p}{2} = 5$ (c) $\frac{p}{5} = 5$ (d) $\frac{p}{2} = 9$

$x = 7, a = 4, m = 6, p = 6, x = 6, a = 0.5$

27

A3 Here are some algebraic expressions and explanations.
Link them together to tell the 'story' of solving an equation.
The first one has already been done.

(a) $3 + x = 7 - x$
[1] (adding x to each side) [2] $x = 2$ [3] (dividing each side by 2)
[4] (subtracting 3 from each side) [5] $3 + 2x = 7$
[6] $2x = 4$

Answer: [5]⟷[1]
[6]⟷[4]
[2]⟷[3]

(b) $2x - 6 = x - 4$
[1] (adding 6 to each side) [2] $x - 6 = {}^-4$
[3] (subtracting x from each side) [4] $x = 2$

(c) $5x - 4 = 2x + 5$
[1] (dividing each side by 3) [2] $3x = 9$
[3] (adding 4 to each side) [4] $x = 3$
[5] (subtracting $2x$ from each side) [6] $5x = 2x + 9$

(d) $2p - 3 = {}^-p + 9$
[1] (dividing each side by 3) [2] $3p - 3 = 9$
[3] (adding 3 to each side) [4] $p = 4$
[5] (adding p to each side) [6] $3p = 12$

A4 You should always check your solutions by substituting them back into the original equation to ensure that 'the left-hand side = right-hand side'.
Here are some equations and three solutions – only one of which is correct. Show which is the correct one by substitution.

(a) $\frac{x}{2} + 2x = x + 6$ [$x = 3, 4$ or 5] (b) $5x - 4 = 2x + 8$ [$x = 4, 6$ or 8]
(c) $5x + 1 = x + 3$ [$x = \frac{1}{4}, \frac{1}{2}$ or $\frac{3}{4}$] (d) $3(2m - 1) = 4 + 5m$ [$m = 5, 6$ or 7]

B1 Solve these equations by inspection.

(a) $4r = 8$ (b) $6s = 3$ (c) $5p = 25$ (d) $q + 2 = 7$
(e) $\frac{z}{2} = 4$ (f) $\frac{m}{3} = 4$ (g) $8n = 64$ (h) $8n = 2$
(i) $12 - x = 8$ (j) $y - 12 = 8$ (k) $y - 4 = 8$ (l) $4 - y = 0$

B2 Solve these equations. Show how you have checked the solutions by substitution.

(a) $2x + 3 = 7$ (b) $2(1 + 2x) - 3 = 7 - 5 + x$ (c) $\frac{r}{6} = 12$
(d) $2x - 7 = x - 4$ (e) $2x + 3 = 9$ (f) $x + x + x - 2 = 2x + 7$

B3 Solve these equations.
  (a) $p - 5 = 2p - 9$ (Hint: this is the same as $2p - 9 = p - 5$.)
  (b) $x + 9 = 3x - 3$ (c) $3w - 4 = 2 - 3w$ (d) $5y - 6 = 16 - 6y$
  (e) $3(q + 1) = 2q$ (f) $49 - 3z = z + 21$ (g) $2n + 14 = 5n + 5$

C1 Solve these equations and check each answer by substituting back into the equation.
  (a) $2x + 9 = 5x + 3$ (b) $8a + 3 = 21 + 5a$ (c) $5m - 3 = 7 + 3m$
  (d) $6z - 1 = 2z$ (e) $5s = 7s - 4$ (f) $9n + 2 = 3n + 20$

C2 Here is a formula for simple equations
   $ax = bx + c$
  where a, b and c represent numbers.
  So in the case of $6x = 2x + 10$, $a = 6$, $b = 2$ and $c = 10$.
  (a) For each of these equations write down the values represented by a, b and c.
    i) $6x = 2x + 20$ ii) $3x = 9$
    iii) $5x = x + 7$ iv) $2x = x + 1$
  (b) Solve the simple equations where
    i) $a = 10$, $b = 8$ and $c = 8$ ii) $a = 11$, $b = 9$ and $c = 8$.
  (c) Investigate one of these by selecting some values of a, b and c of your own.
    i) How do the solutions change with different values of c when a and b are kept the same?
    ii) For values of a and b which have the same difference how do the values of c affect the solution?

C3 Here is an activity that Sanjay used to help him practise solving equations.
  He used an ordinary 6-sided dice. First he drew this on a piece of plain paper.

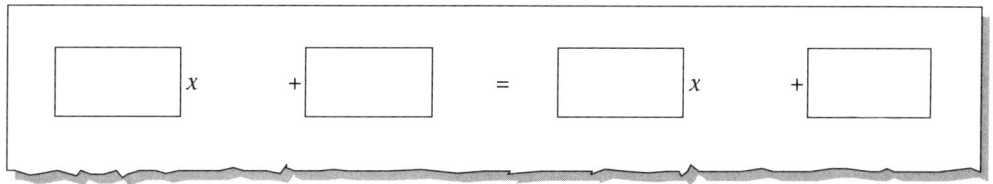

  The four numbers which fit into the boxes are found by throwing the dice four times. He tried to solve the resulting equation. Try the activity for yourself.
  Make up a game of it by taking it in turns to make and solve an equation.
  The winner is the player with the larger solution.
  What is (a) the largest and (b) the smallest possible solution?
  Make up a game like this one for yourself.

10 Solving problems with algebra

Key ideas

Following these five steps will help solve most problems involving using algebra.

- Read through the question or problem several times.
  (*Drawing a rough diagram or table can sometimes help.*)
- Decide what needs to be found – the unknown – and which letter you will use to represent this unknown.
  (*Always state this in your working, for example, 'Let x be Sue's height in cm … .'*)
- Use the information to form two expressions which are equal. At least one of these must involve the unknown. As these two expressions are equal they can form either side of an equation.
  (*Be especially careful to make sure that the same units are used throughout, i.e. all in £s or all in ps, not a mixture of the two – which is a common mistake.*)
- Solve the equation.
- Check your solution against **the original information** given in the question.
  (*Look at your solution and ask yourself 'Is this a sensible answer?'.
  For example, answers giving people's heights as 180 metres should be checked!*)

Here is a worked example.
Bill is now twice as old as Neeta. Five years ago the sum of their ages was 32. How old are they now?

Let Neeta be x years old now.
So Bill is now $2x$ years old now.   *'Bill is now twice as old as Neeta.'*
Five years ago Neeta was $(x - 5)$ and Bill was $(2x - 5)$ years old.
But *'five years ago the sum of their ages was 32.'*
$$\text{So } (x - 5) + (2x - 5) = 32$$
$$3x - 10 = 32$$
$$\text{so } x = 14$$
Neeta is now 14 and Bill is 28.   *'Bill is now twice as old as Neeta.'*

Check
  If Bill is now 28 and Neeta is 14 – *'Bill is now twice as old as Neeta.'* ✓
  Five years ago their ages were 23 and 9, which sum to 32 –
  'Five years ago the sum of their ages was 32.' ✓
The answers are consistent with the original information.

A1 Write these statements, about a number x, as mathematical expressions.

(a) The sum of 6 and the number.
(b) One less than double the number.
(c) Three more than the number.
(d) The product of the number and 7.
(e) The number increased by 9.
(f) Five decreased by the number.
(g) Two more than twice the number.
(h) Six less than the number.

A2 Tasneem is 5 years older than Tariq.
In three years time the sum of their ages will be 21.

(a) Copy and complete this table.

	Age now (years)	Age in 3 years time
Tariq	x	
Tasneem		

(b) Use the table to help you find what age Tasneem and Tariq are now.

A3 Five added to twice a number gives an answer of 13.
Set up and solve an equation to find this number.

A4 Six subtracted from the product of four and a number gives an answer of 22.
What is the number?

A5 The length of a rectangular field is 10 metres more than its width.
The perimeter of the field is 220 metres.
What are the width and length of the field? (Hint: a rough sketch may help.)

A6 A rectangle measures $(2x + 1)$ cm by $(x + 9)$ cm.
Find the value of x for which the rectangle is a square.

A7 The three sides of a triangle, in centimetres, are $(x + 4)$, $(x + 6)$ and $(2x - 6)$.

(a) What values of x will produce an isosceles triangle?
(b) Is it possible to have a value of x which will produce an equilateral triangle? Explain your answer.

A8 There are two squares. One has sides x centimetres long, the other has sides which are $(x + 90)$ millimetres long.
Find the value of x for which both squares will have the same area.

B1 Reva thought of a number, multiplied it by three and then subtracted five. The answer was 10. Write down and solve an equation to find the number that she thought of.

B2 Dena read a new book. It had 96 pages and took her seven days.
She read x pages on each of the first five days.
On the sixth day she read 10 pages and on the last day she read 6 pages.
Write down and solve an equation to find the value of x.

B3 Martin thought of a number, multiplied it by ten and then added five. The answer was 80. Write down and solve an equation to find the number that he thought of.

B4 The perimeter of a triangle is 13 cm. The sides are $2x$ cm, x cm and 4 cm long. Write down and solve an equation to find the value of x.

B5 Here in words and in 'algebra' is a partly finished 'think of a number' problem.
  (a) i) Copy it out and complete it.

Instructions in words	Algebraic expression
Think of any number	Let x be any number
Multiply it by two	$2x$
Add 5	$2x + 5$
Multiply by five	...
Subtract twenty-five	...
Divide by ten	...

  ii) What do you notice about the final entry?
  Ask some people to work through the instructions.
  What is their final number?

  (b) i) Copy and complete this 'think of a number' problem.

Instructions in words	Algebraic expression
Think of any number	Let x be any number
...	$5x$
...	$5x + 5$
Divide by 5	$x + 1$
Take away the number you first thought of	...

  ii) What do you notice about the final entry?
  Ask some people to work through the instructions.

  (c) Make up and test some similar 'think of a number' tricks for yourself.

B6 In a triangle the angles are $x°$, $(2x + 10)°$ and $(3x + 20)°$.
Form an equation in x and solve it to find the three angles of the triangle.

C1 Jordan is x years old. His sister Sophie is 4 years older. Their mother is twice as old as the total of their ages. The sum of all three people's ages is 72 years. How old is each of the three people?

C2 Anita orders a glass of fruit juice costing x pence and a jacket potato costing £1.80 more. She pays with a £10 note and receives £7 change.
Form an equation involving x and use it to find the cost of:
(a) a fruit juice and (b) a jacket potato.

C3 Chloe only has 5p and 50p coins in her money box.
She has twice as many 50p coins as 5p coins.
The total amount of money in her money box is £10.50.
Let there be x 5p coins and use this to find the number of (a) 5p and (b) 50p coins in Chloe's money box.

C4 (a) If x is an odd number what is the next larger odd number?
(b) Three times the larger of two consecutive odd numbers is 17 more than the sum of the two numbers. Find the two numbers.

C5 There are two numbers whose sum is 39.
Three times the first is 5 more than the second.
What are the two numbers?

C6 Amy, Beth and Carla all collect CDs. They have 198 CDs between them. Amy has 6 times more CDs than Beth, and Carla has 2 times more CDs than Beth. How many CDs does each person have?

C7 Marie and Paula each have some money.
Marie started off with £10 more than Paula.
Paula managed to double her money and Marie increased hers by £20.
They now find that they both have the same amount of money.
How much money did each person start with?
Show clearly how you arrived at your answer.

11 Inequalities

Key ideas

The '=' symbol shows two expressions to be equal, for example $2x + 2 = x + 8$.
(The expression '$2x + 2$' *is equal to* the expression '$x + 8$'.)
There are other symbols describing relationships between expressions.
Here are some of them; these are called inequalities.

>   'greater than'   ≥   'greater than or equal to'
<   'less than'   ≤   'less than or equal to'

You need to learn these symbols.

The inequality $x \leq 2$ means that x can have any value less than or equal to 2, for example, 1, 0, ⁻1.5, ⁻9.9, … Similarly the inequality $x > ⁻6$ means that x can have any value greater than (but not equal to) ⁻6, for example, ⁻5.7, ⁻3, 0, 999, …
Note, for example, that $x > ⁻6$ could also be written $⁻6 < x$.

Inequalities can be combined. For example, $⁻6 < x \leq 2$ means that x can have any value greater than ⁻6 which is up to but not equal to 2.
Inequalities can be shown on a number line (or **number line graph**). For example,

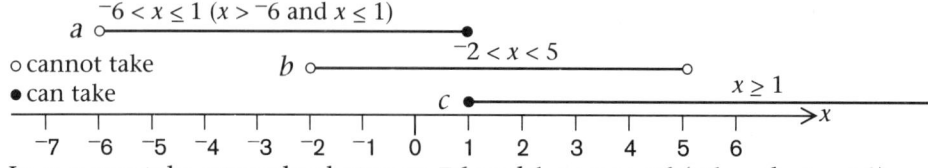

In *a*, x can take any value between ⁻6 and 1 except ⁻6 ($⁻6 < x$ but $x \leq 1$).
In *b*, x can take any value between ⁻2 and 5 except ⁻1 or 5 ($⁻1 < x$ and $x < 5$).
In *c*, x can take any value greater than and including 1.

Balancing – treating both sides of the equation in the same way – which is used to solve equations, can also be used to solve inequalities.
For example, solving the inequality $3x + 2 < 14$

$$3x < 14 - 2 \quad \text{(taking 2 from each side)}$$
$$\text{so} \quad 3x < 12$$
$$\text{and} \quad x < 4 \quad \text{(dividing both sides by 3)}$$

Just as with equations, it's a good idea to check your solution by substituting back into the original inequality. Now for $x < 4$, a value of $x = 2$ is a possible value for x. For this value of x, $3x + 2$ takes the value 8, which is less than 14 (< 14) so $x < 4$ seems to be a reasonable solution.

A1 Write these statements as algebraic expressions.
The first one has been done for you.

(a) The number n is less than 8. $n < 8$ or $8 > n$.

(b) The number m is less than 8 and greater than 4.

(c) The number x is less than or equal to 8 and greater than or equal to 4.

(d) Twice r is greater than or equal to 19.

(e) The sum of x and y is less than 20.

A2 (a) Which of these values of x fit (**satisfy**) $x \leq {}^-2$?

i) $^-1$ ii) 1 iii) 0 iv) $^-2$ v) $^-6$

(b) Which of these values of t satisfy $5 \leq t$ and $t > 0$?

i) 5 ii) 3 iii) 1 iv) 0 v) $^-1$

(c) Which of these values of x satisfy $^-2 \leq x$ and $2 > x$?

i) $^-1$ ii) $^-2$ iii) 1 iv) 0 v) 2

A3 Here is a number line together with some inequalities.

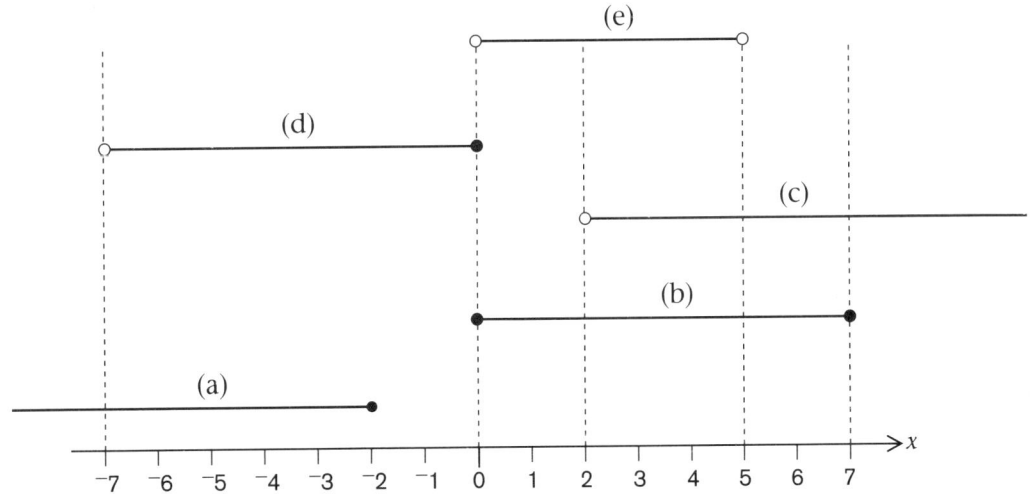

Match each of these algebraic expressions with the lines above.

[1] $0 \leq x \leq 7$ [2] $^-7 < x \leq 0$ [3] $x \leq {}^-2$
[4] $0 < x < 5$ [5] $2 < x$

A4 Show these inequalities on a number line in the same way as in question A3 above.

(a) $x \leq 0$ (b) $x > 0$ (c) $x < {}^-1$ (d) $x \geq {}^-2$

A5 Write two possible whole number **solutions** for these inequalities.

(a) $n \geq 1$ (b) $p < 4$ (c) $q \geq {}^-1$ (d) $w > {}^-4$

B1 Write all the possible whole number solutions for the following.

(a) $3 \leq x < 6$ (b) $3 < x < 6$ (c) $3 < x \leq 6$ (d) $3 \leq x \leq 6$

Check your answers by using a number line, similar to that in question A3.

B2 Write algebraic expressions to describe the inequalities shown on these number lines.

(a)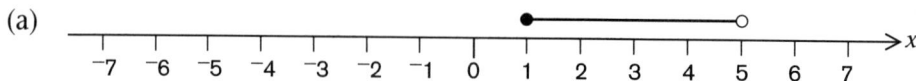

(b)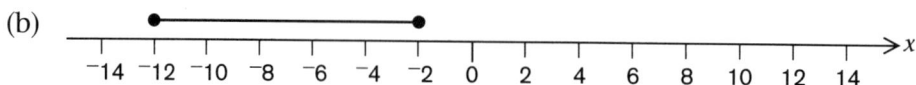

(c)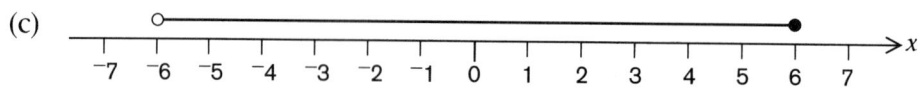

(d)

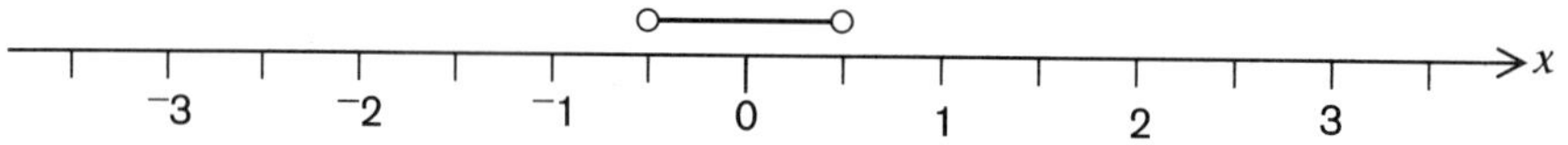

B3 Solve these inequalities.

(a) $x + 2 \geq 10$ (b) $z + 5 < 7$ (c) $v + 10 > 6$ (d) $2y + 3 \leq 13$

(e) $2k - 3 > 11$ (f) $4p + 3 > 19$ (g) $7x + 3 < 5x + 9$

B4 Match the tables of values with the inequalities.

[1] $2x - y > 0$
[2] $x < y$
[3] $x \leq y$
[4] $3x + y > 12$

Table A

x	y
0	0
1	1
2	2

Table B

x	y
1	5
2	3
4	6

Table C

x	y
1	1
3	5
5	3

Table D

x	y
3	6
4	6
6	3

C1 Here is a game for you to play. You will need a dice.
- Write down a number between 1 and 6.
- To the right of the number write down an inequality symbol of your choice.
- Now throw the dice.
  If the number fits the inequality you win a point, and so on.

5 < ?

Play the game with a friend. Change it to make it more interesting if you wish.

C2 You will need two different-coloured or marked dice for this question.
Algebraic expressions can be used to summarise the winning throws in a dice game.
For ordinary 6-sided dice, let r represent the score on the red dice and b the score on the black dice.

A possible winning rule might be $r = b$, or scores equal on both dice.

Winning rule is $r = b$

r (score on red dice)	b (score on black dice)
1	1
2	2

Another winning rule might be $r + b > 10$, which is the sum of the two scores greater than 10, and so on.
In a table write down *all* the winning throws with red and black dice which fit these rules.
(a) $2r + b < 8$ (b) $r + b \geq 10$ (c) $r - b > 4$
Make up some similar rules and play the resulting game with a friend.

C3 Here are some supposed winning rules for ordinary 6-sided dice (see question C2). Which are impossible to ever satisfy? Give a reason for each one.
(a) $r + b \leq 2$ (b) $2r + b < 3$ (c) $r > 12 - b$ (d) $2r + 3b \geq 30$
(e) Why wouldn't the rule $2r + 3b \geq 5$ be much use?

C4 Solve these inequalities and for each one write down a possible whole number value for the **unknown** which satisfies the solution.
(a) $x + 2 > {}^-2$ (b) $5 \geq x - 3$ (c) $6 < x - 3$
(d) ${}^-5 > x - 3$ (e) $5x + 1 \leq 11$ (f) $10 + 3x \leq 5x + 4$

12 Decimal practice

You should do this unit without using a calculator.

A1 In the number 263 (= 200 + 60 + 3), the 2 represents 2 hundreds, the 6 represents 6 tens and the 3 represents 3 ones.
Write down the value represented by 6 in each of these numbers.
(a) 761 (b) 6123 (c) 106 (d) 0.6 (e) 0.06 (f) 1.61

A2 Here are some scales. Write down the numbers that these arrows point to.

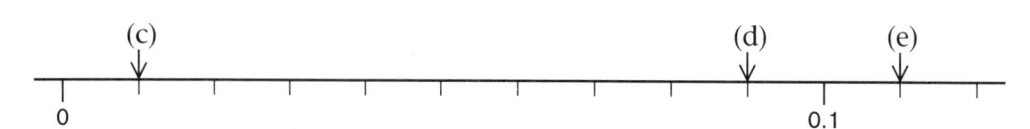

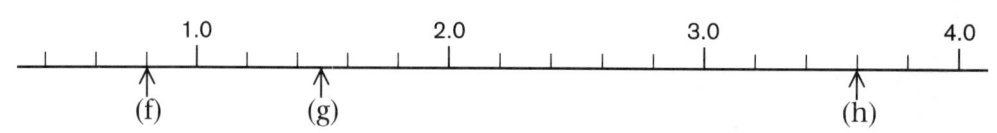

A3 Write these fractions as decimals.
(a) $\frac{4}{10}$ (b) $\frac{4}{100}$ (c) $\frac{40}{100}$ (d) $1\frac{1}{2}$ (e) $1\frac{1}{4}$

A4 Calculate these. (Remember no calculator is allowed – try to do them in your head.)
(a) 2.1 + 1.2 (b) 4.3 + 0.1 (c) 3.1 − 2.1 (d) 4.7 − 0.3
(e) 21.3 − 3.0 (f) 0.4 + 0.6 + 1 (g) 12.3 − 0.4 (h) 1.6 + 2.0 + 0.4

A5 (a) Rewrite these measurements in centimetres.
   i) 50 mm ii) 35 mm iii) 1.2 m iv) 1.02 m
(b) Rewrite these measurements in millimetres.
   i) 2 cm ii) 5.2 cm iii) 2.1 m iv) 0.02 cm

B1 This table gives the weights of vitamins and minerals per 100g of Sultana Bran Flakes.

Vitamin or mineral	Weight in g per 100g of Sultana Bran Flakes
Folic acid	0.000280
Iron	0.0098
Niacin	0.0126
Pantothenic acid	0.0042
Sodium	0.5
Vitamin B6	0.0014
Vitamin B1	0.001
Vitamin B12	0.0000007
Vitamin B2	0.0011
Vitamin D	0.0000035

Write the weights in order, starting with the smallest.

B2 Write the following as decimals.
(a) six and one tenth
(b) six hundredths
(c) sixty hundredths
(d) one and one hundredths
(e) one thousandth
(f) twenty-one tenths

B3 Work these out.
(a) 8.6 + 3.75 + 5.02
(b) 18.9 − 13.6
(c) 0.59 − 0.38
(d) 3.29 + 142
(e) 2.5 − 1.6
(f) 102.03 − 37.38

B4 In a diving competition Lucy, who won, scored 60.1, 49.9 and 47.5 points. Emily came second with 46.9, 51.8 and 55.4 points.
(a) Calculate the total score of each diver.
(b) By how much did Lucy win?

B5 Find the values of the following.
(a) £2.67 + 184p
(b) £24 − 758p
(c) £123.10 − £9.99

B6 Round off these sums of money to the nearest penny.
(a) £4.5199
(b) £12.901
(c) £0.123
(d) £2.9909

C1 The object of this activity is to practise estimating with decimals. You will need some plain paper – the unused sides of worksheets will do.

Sketch a grid like the one here, with values of x and y going from 0 to 1. Now plot these points as accurately as you can by estimating. When you join up each set of points they make a shape; remember to join the final line to the start. Write down the name of each shape.

(a) (0.5, 0.3) (0.7, 0.5) (0.9, 0.3) (0.7, 0.1)

(b) (0, 0.7) (0.2, 0.9) (0.4, 0.9) (0.5, 0.7)

(c) (0.2, 0.1) (0.1, 0.2) (0.6, 0.7) (0.7, 0.6)

(d) (0.2, 0.1) (0.5, 1.0) (0.8, 0.1) (0.5, 0.4)

Make up some similar puzzles for yourself.
You might be adventurous and have x and y values ranging from zero to 0.01!

C2 For very small masses we sometimes use the milligram, written mg, which is one thousandth of a gram. Another small unit used is the microgram which is written as µg and is one millionth of a gram.

Here is a table showing the nutritional composition per 100g of Cheddar and cottage cheese. Use the table to answer the questions below. Give your answers in grams (g) – not milligrams (mg) or micrograms (µg).

	Water (g)	Protein (g)	Fat (g)	Carbohydrate (g)	Minerals calcium (mg)	iron (mg)	A (µg)	B1 (mg)	Vitamins B2 (mg)	niacin (mg)	C (mg)	D (µg)
Cheddar cheese	37	26.0	33.5	0	800	0.4	412	0.04	0.50	6.2	0	0.26
Cottage cheese	79	13.6	4.0	1.4	60	0.1	41	0.02	0.19	3.3	0	0.2

(a) How many grams of calcium are there in a 100g piece of Cheddar cheese?

(b) How many grams of vitamin A are there in 100g of cottage cheese?

(c) How many more grams of vitamin D are there in 100g of Cheddar cheese than in 100g of cottage cheese?

(d) In a 1kg piece of Cheddar cheese how much, in grams, is:

i) water   ii) calcium   iii) vitamin A   iv) iron?

⓭ Multiplication with decimals

Key ideas

There are several methods for multiplying decimals.
Here are a few – make sure you understand how each method works.
You may have method(s) of your own (apart from using a calculator!) – don't worry – use the method *you* feel happiest with.

(Whole number) × (Decimal number less than 1)

(a) 6×0.09
  $= 6 \times 9$ hundredths
  $= 54$ hundredths
  $= 0.54$

(b) 6×0.09
  $= (6 \times 0.9) \div 10$
  $= (6 \times 9) \div 100$
  $= 54 \div 100$
  $= 0.54$

(Whole number) × (Decimal number)

(c) 6.3×8 (or 8×6.3)
  $= (8 \times 6 \text{ ones}) + (8 \times 3 \text{ tenths})$
  $= 48 \text{ ones} + 24 \text{ tenths}$
  $= 48 + 2.4$
  $= 50.4$

(d) $6.3 \times 8 \approx 6 \times 8 = 48$
  (a rough answer)
  $63 \times 8 = 504$ ('forgetting' the decimal point)
  From the rough answer we know that the correct answer is round about 48,
  so $6.3 \times 8 = 50.4$

(Decimal number) × (Decimal number)

(e) 6.8×2.4
  $\approx 7 \times 3 = 21$ (approximate answer)
  but $68 \times 24 = 1632$ (ignoring decimal points and using your own method of multiplying two whole numbers)
  so $6.8 \times 2.4 = 16.32$

(f) 6.8×2.4
  $= (0.1 \times 68) \times (0.1 \times 24)$
  $= (0.1 \times 0.1) \times (68 \times 24)$
  $= 0.01 \times 1632$
  $= 16.32$

Remember that the order of a multiplication has no effect on the answer, so, for example, $2.3 \times 54 = 54 \times 2.3$.

A1 Look carefully at these three calculation patterns.
(a) Write down the next row of the table.

1 × 1 = 1	0.1 × 1 = 0.1	0.01 × 1 = 0.01
1 × 0.1 = 0.1	0.1 × 0.1 = 0.01	0.01 × 0.1 = 0.001
1 × 0.01 = 0.01	0.1 × 0.01 = 0.001	0.01 × 0.01 = 0.0001

(b) Copy and complete this pattern of calculations.

5 × 6 = 30	0.5 × 6 = ?	0.05 × 6 = 0.3
5 × 0.6 = ?	0.5 × 0.6 = ?	0.05 × 0.6 = ?
5 × 0.06 = 0.3	0.5 × 0.06 = ?	0.05 × 0.06 = ?

A2 Copy and complete these calculations.

(a) 8 × 0.04
 = 8 × _____ hundredths
 = _____ hundredths
 = _____

(b) 0.012 × 4
 = 4 × 0.012
 = 4 × _____ thousandths
 = _____ thousandths
 = _____

(c) 12.1 × 0.9 ≈ _____ × _____
 121 × 9 = 1089
 so 12.1 × 0.9 = _____

A3 Work these out without using a calculator.
(a) 6 × 4.2 (b) 5.1 × 8 (c) 1.06 × 6
(d) 6.9 × 0.2 (e) 1.1 × 90 (f) 1.9 × 2.1 (19 × 21 = 399)

Check your answers with a calculator.

A4 Use these multiplication 'facts' to work out the calculations below.
 27 × 95 = 2565   45 × 32 = 1440   36 × 82 = 2952

(a) 0.32 × 45 (b) 36 × 0.82 (c) 0.82 × 360
(d) 27 × 9.5 (e) 2.7 × 9.5 (f) 45 × 3.2
(g) 4.5 × 3.2 (h) 0.27 × 95 (i) 3.6 × 8.2

B1 Work these out without using a calculator.
    (a)   9.7 × 2   (b)   0.97 × 2   (c)   0.97 × 0.2   (d)   0.097 × 0.2
    (e)   2.25 × 4   (f)   2.25 × 0.4   (g)   2.25 × 0.04   (h)   0.225 × 0.04
Use a calculator to check your answers.

B2 Work these out without using a calculator.
    (a)   225 × 10   (b)   22.5 × 10   (c)   2.25 × 10   (d)   0.225 × 10
    (e)   225 × 20   (f)   22.5 × 20   (g)   2.25 × 20   (h)   0.225 × 20
Use a calculator to check your answers.

B3 Find the cost of these. Give your answer in £s – don't use a calculator.
    (a)   4 books at £2.25 each
    (b)   8 bars of chocolate at £0.65 each
    (c)   2.5 kg of new potatoes at £0.80 per kg
Use a calculator to check your answers.

B4 Use the fact that 6.27 × 0.12 = 0.7524 to write down the answers to:
    (a)   627 × 0.12   (b)   6.27 × 1.2   (c)   12 × 6.27   (d)   12 × 627

C1 Use pencil and paper to work out 145 × 23. Use your answer to find:
    (a)   14.5 × 23   (b)   1.45 × 2.3   (c)   0.145 × 23   (d)   14.5 × 2.3

C2 Use the fact that 73.6 × 45 = 3312 to write down at least six multiplications, which involve decimals and which have 3312 as their answer.

C3 Holly found this in an old book of arithmetic 'short cuts'.
    0.03 × 0.2 = 0.006 [2 decimal places + 1 decimal place gives 3 decimal places]
    2.25 × 0.037 = 0.08325 [2 decimal places + 3 decimal places gives 5 decimal places]
Try to work out what the method is – does it work? Experiment!

14 Division with decimals

Key ideas

There are several methods for dividing numbers involving decimals. Here are a few – make sure you understand how each method works. You may have method(s) of your own (apart from using a calculator!) – don't worry – use the method *you* feel happiest with.

(Decimal number) ÷ (Whole number)

(a)   3.7 ÷ 4

$$4 \overline{\smash{)}3.7}$$
$$0.$$

3 ÷ 4 'won't go'

$$4 \overline{\smash{)}3.7}$$
$$0.9$$

3 ones are 'worth' 30 tenths
and (30 + 7) tenths ÷ 4 = 9
tenths with 1 tenth left

$$4 \overline{\smash{)}3.7^{10}}$$
$$0.92$$

1 tenth is 'worth' 10 hundredths
10 hundredths ÷ 4
= 2 hundredths with 2 hundredths left

$$4 \overline{\smash{)}3.7^{10\ 20}}$$
$$0.925$$

2 hundredths are worth 20 thousandths
20 thousandths ÷ 4
= 5 thousandths so 3.7 ÷ 4 = 0.925.

(b)   3.7 ÷ 4 ≈ 1   approximate answer

   37 ÷ 4 = 9.25   ignoring the decimal point

   so 3.7 ÷ 4 = 0.925.

> *(Decimal number) ÷ (Decimal number)*
>
> (c) Treating both sides of the division in the same way does not alter the answer. For example, with 40 ÷ 5, multiply both sides by 3
>
> $$= (40 \times 3) \div (5 \times 3)$$
> $$= 120 \div 15$$
> $$= 8$$
>
> $4.85 \div 0.5$
> $= (4.85 \times 10) \div (0.5 \times 10)$ to divide by a whole number 5
> $= 48.5 \div 5$
> $= 9.7$ using your own method for decimal ÷ whole number.
>
> By the same method:
> $4.8 \div 0.4$
> $= (4.8 \times 10) \div (0.4 \times 10)$
> $= 48 \div 4$
> $= 12.$

Try not to use a calculator for any of the questions – apart from checking.

A1 (a) $3.72 \div 3$ (b) $3.65 \div 5$ (c) $0.075 \div 5$ (d) $1.84 \div 8$
   (e) $18.4 \div 8$ (f) $66.84 \div 4$ (g) $0.0372 \div 6$ (h) $11.07 \div 9$

A2 (a) $5.2 \div 0.4$ (b) $3.5 \div 0.2$ (c) $6 \div 1.2$ (d) $0.128 \div 0.4$
   (e) $1.07 \div 0.1$ (f) $0.5 \div 0.2$ (g) $0.72 \div 1.2$ (h) $7.12 \div 0.01$

A3 (a) $868 \div 0.2$ (b) $0.432 \div 0.3$ (c) $81.2 \div 0.4$ (d) $5.35 \div 0.05$
   (e) $25.2 \div 0.12$ (f) $5.16 \div 1.2$ (g) $0.322 \div 1.4$ (h) $0.035 \div 0.005$

A4 (a) A plank of wood is 3.84 m long. If it is to be cut into six identical pieces how long will each of these pieces of wood be?

   (b) An ordinary wine bottle holds 0.75 litres of wine. How many of these bottles would be needed to hold 9 litres of wine?

B1 Use the 'fact' that 1120 ÷ 32 = 35 to write down the answers to these.

(a) 112 ÷ 32 (b) 11.2 ÷ 3.2 (c) 112 ÷ 320

(d) 1.12 ÷ 32 (e) 112 ÷ 0.32 (f) 1120 ÷ 0.032

B2 Here are some calculations. Which have the same answers?

(a) 945 ÷ 35 (b) 94.5 ÷ 35 (c) 9.45 ÷ 0.35

(d) 94.5 ÷ 3.5 (e) 0.945 ÷ 0.35 (f) 945 ÷ 350

B3 Double-sided tape used to fit carpets costs £1.92 for 12 metres.
Find the cost of this tape per metre.

B4 A rough rule for converting speeds in miles per hour into speeds in km per hour is to divide the speed in miles per hour by 0.6.
Change these speeds into km per hour.

(a) Speed skating record at 27 m.p.h.
(b) Fastest recorded tennis serve of 138 m.p.h.
(c) Fastest recorded speed of a train in normal service, the French TGV, with a speed of 321 m.p.h.

C1 Here is a table showing how to convert some old Imperial units to their metric equivalents.

To change	into	divide by
inches	millimetres	0.04
miles	kilometres	0.6
pounds	kilograms	2.2
gallons	litres	0.2

Use the table to change these measurements into their metric equivalents.

(a) 1.6 inches (b) 8 gallons (c) 1.5 miles (d) 154 pounds

C2 Here are the prices of some different amounts of peach oil.

Bottle	Volume of oil (ml)	Cost (£)
A	1.3	1.95
B	1.2	1.86
C	1.5	2.40

Assuming that it is the same oil in each bottle, which bottle gives you 'most oil for your money'?

Show all your working – don't just guess!

15 In your head 1

You may find it useful to have someone read these questions to you.
To build up speed ask them to read the question once only.
Aim to answer each question in 10 seconds.

A1 About how many kilograms is ten pounds?
A2 What number is exactly half-way between zero point one and zero point two?
A3 If x takes a value of five, what is the value of six x?
A4 Fifty pence pieces have a mass of thirteen point five grams.
    What will ten fifty pence pieces weigh?
A5 What length of fencing will be needed to fence in a square field of side sixty metres?
A6 Two angles of a triangle add up to one hundred and twenty-five degrees.
    How many degrees is the third angle?
A7 What is the sum of zero point six and zero point eight?
A8 List all the prime numbers between thirty and forty.
A9 Jade needs thirty-three carpet tiles for her new flat.
    Carpet tiles are sold in boxes of ten. How many boxes does she need to buy?
A10 What is the area, in square centimetres, of a rectangle measuring nine centimetres by seven centimetres?

B1 How many days are there in twelve weeks?
B2 What change is left from ten pounds after spending one pound twenty-five?
B3 What is a quarter of one hundred and twenty?
B4 How many millilitres are there in one and a quarter litres?
B5 Write in figures the number which is zero point one five less than ten.
B6 What is the product of sixty-one and five?
B7 How many hours is four hundred and twenty minutes?
B8 What is the sum of one, two, three, four and five?
B9 Jot down an approximate answer to six point one multiplied by four point eight.
B10 What must be added to twenty-three to make ninety?

16 In your head 2

You may find it useful to have someone read these questions to you.
To build up speed ask them to read the question once only.
Aim to answer each question in 10 seconds.

A1 About how many kilometres is ten miles?
A2 A pair of jeans cost thirty pounds. Their price was reduced by ten per cent. What is the new price?
A3 If x takes a value of five, what is the value of a half of x?
A4 Write down the difference between sixty-one and one point nine.
A5 Write one quarter as a decimal.
A6 Write down two fractions which are equivalent to zero point two.
A7 What is three quarters of one hundred pounds?
A8 What is sixteen multiplied by four?
A9 How many vertices does an octagon have?
A10 In an isosceles triangle one angle is one hundred degrees. What is the size of one of the other angles?

B1 How many hours are there in three days?
B2 The sum of two numbers is nine.
    Their product is twenty.
    What are the two numbers?
B3 The mean of two numbers is ten. One of the numbers is twelve. What is the other number?
B4 What is twenty per cent of ten pounds?
B5 Write down one tenth of six hundred and fifty-six.
B6 What is three point two added to zero point three?
B7 Multiply twenty-five by seven.
B8 What is twelve thousand shared by six?
B9 Three times a is twelve. What is the value of two times a?
B10 What must be added to zero point nine two to make two?

Extensions

1 Algebra practice 1

1.1 Here is an example of a number triangle. The sum of the numbers along each side is the same.

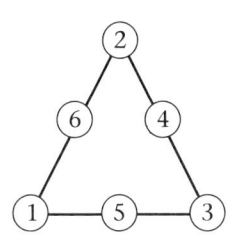

(a) Copy and complete this number triangle.

(b) Copy and complete these algebraic 'number' triangles.

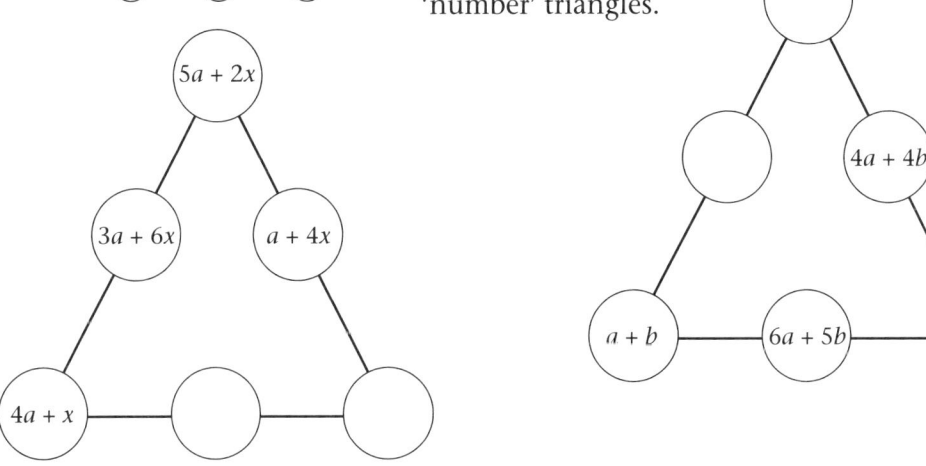

1.2 Draw four boxes in a line.

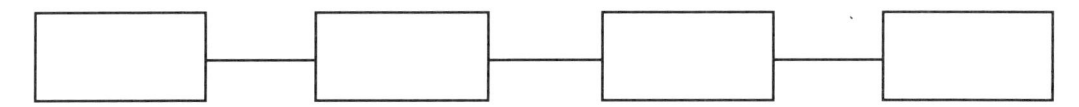

Choose two numbers. Write them in the first two boxes.
In the third box put the sum of the numbers of the previous two boxes.
In the fourth box put the sum of the numbers of the previous two boxes.
Add the numbers in the first and fourth boxes.

Compare your answer with the number in the third box. What do you notice?

Try to explain the result by representing the numbers in the first and second box by a and b.

2 Algebra practice 2

2.1 Here is the complete set of dominoes up to a double two.

There is a formula giving the total number of dominoes needed to make a full set up to double n.

There is also one giving the total number of spots in a double n set of dominoes.

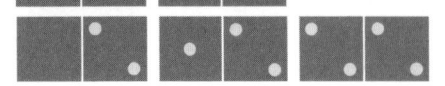

Below are some possible formulas.

Investigate which formulas are the correct ones for each situation. Explain how you arrived at your answer.

$\frac{(n+1)(n+2)}{2}$ $\frac{3n^2}{2}$ $\frac{n(4n+4)}{2}$ $3n^2$ $(n+1)(n+2)$

$2n(n+1)$ $\frac{n(n+1)(n+2)}{2}$ n^2+2 $\frac{n(n+1)(n+2)}{4}$

2.2 (a) Show that this is a 4 by 4 magic square.

(b) What is special about the 4 by 4 magic square in which

$A = 0, B = 30, C = 60, D = 90$

$a = 13, b = 23, c = 41, d = 67$?

(c) What is special about the 4 by 4 magic square in which

$A = 0, B = 12, C = 8, D = 4$

$a = 4, b = 1, c = 2, d = 3$?

$A+a$	$D+c$	$C+b$	$B+d$
$C+d$	$B+b$	$A+c$	$D+a$
$B+c$	$C+a$	$D+d$	$A+b$
$D+b$	$A+d$	$B+a$	$C+c$

2.3 This diagram shows two rulers placed side by side.

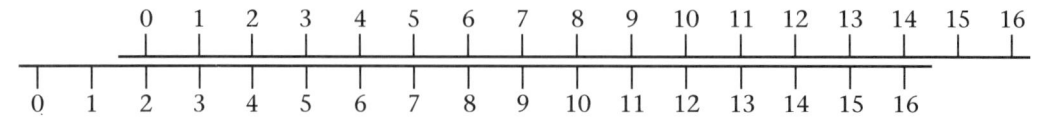

As you can see, the numbers line up.

Write down an algebraic rule connecting the top scale numbers (t) with the bottom scale numbers (b). How could such a simple device be used to work out additions and subtractions, including negative numbers? Try to use algebra to help you.

3 Probability 1

3.1 Jim will not walk to school because, he says,
'Two outcomes may occur. I can be abducted by aliens or I won't be abducted by aliens. There are only two outcomes – abducted or not abducted. So there is a 50% chance or probability of $\frac{1}{2}$ being abducted by aliens – I'm not going in!'
What is wrong with Jim's probability calculation?

3.2 Many people think that a six is hard to get with a 6-sided dice, harder than any other number. The reason for this is very simple: when we are waiting for a six we are unconsciously comparing the probability of getting a six with the probability of not getting a six. The first event has a probability of $\frac{1}{6}$ and the second a probability of $\frac{5}{6}$.
Carry out a survey among your friends to see if any think a 6 is harder to get than any other number. Try to convince any who do think this that they are wrong!

3.3 Here is a question from a text book.

> There are 6 cars on a garage forecourt: 3 of them are red, 2 of them are black and 1 is white. What is the probability that the first one to be sold is:
> (a) a black one (b) not a black one (c) a red one (d) a blue one?

Look carefully at the question.

(a) As it stands it can't really be answered. What needs to be added?

(b) Once part (a) has been added answer the original question yourself.

4 Probability 2

4.1 These dominoes are the pick-up pile, so they are face down on the table.

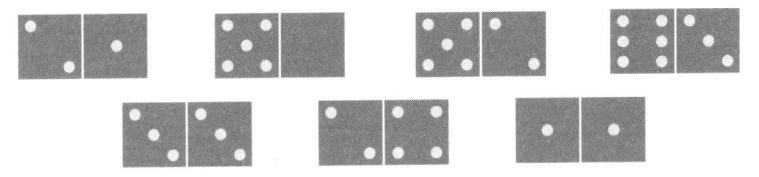

It is Amy's turn to pick up.
She does this by picking one of the dominoes at random.

What is the probability that Amy picks up a domino with

(a) a 2 on it (b) not a 2 on it

(c) a 5 on it (d) not a 5 on it?

(e) She needs to pick up a 2 or a 5 to win.

Is the probability of doing this $\frac{4}{7}$ or $\frac{5}{7}$?

Think carefully and explain your choice carefully.

(f) The person about to pick up here needs a 2 or a 3 to win.

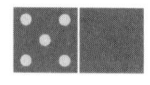

According to Mark the probability of winning is $\frac{4}{4}$ or 1.
Why is Mark wrong and what is the correct answer?

4.2 One of the oldest dice games played in Europe is called Hazard.
The game is over 500 years old. It involves throwing three 6-sided dice.
The scores on each of these are then added to give the total.
Up until about the time of Galileo it was thought that the probability of getting a total of ten was the same as getting a total of 9.
Several old books on dice games gave the six ways of getting each total as:

10 = 1 + 3 + 6 = 1 + 4 + 5 = 2 + 2 + 6 = 2 + 3 + 5 = 2 + 4 + 4 = 3 + 3 + 4 and

9 = 1 + 2 + 6 = 1 + 3 + 5 = 1 + 4 + 4 = 2 + 2 + 5 = 2 + 3 + 4 = 3 + 3 + 3.

But gamblers knew from experience that a total of 10 was slightly more likely to occur. Galileo agreed, he found that a total of 10 could occur in 27 ways – not 6. How many ways did he (correctly) find that 9 could occur?

4.3 You may have played this old playground game.
You count to three and then make one of these shapes with your fist:
open hand (paper), two fingers (scissors) or a fist (stone).
The winner is decided by these rules:

• stone breaks scissors, scissors cut paper and paper covers stone,
• if both players make the same shape it is a draw.

Play the game a few times with a friend.
Is there a way of increasing your chances of winning (without cheating!)?

(a) To help you, draw up a table of all the possible results.
Here is part of one.
Mark a win for player A with an A,
a win for player B with a B, and mark
a draw with a D.
Use your table to answer this question.

(b) Assuming that both players choose paper, stone or scissors at random, what is the probability of there being a draw?

		Player B		
		scissors	paper	stone
P l a y e r A	scissors			
	paper			
	stone			

4.4 Play this game with a friend.
You each need a coin. One player is 'same' and the other player is 'different'. Decide who is to be which.
Each player flips their coin.
The 'same' player wins if the result is 2 Heads or 2 Tails.
The 'different' player wins if the result is 1 Head and 1 Tail.

Investigate the fairness of the game by listing all the possible outcomes. What do you notice?

'Same'	'Different'	Winner
H	H	Same

5 Probability 3

5.1 Investigate this by experimenting on some friends.
Ask them to choose any two digits in the range 1 to 9.
Calculate the experimental probability that the difference between these two digits is 0, 1, 3, 4, etc. You may be surprised at the results!

5.2 'When people are asked to pick a number in the range 1 to 9.
There is a high probability that they will pick 3 or 7.'
Investigate this statement for yourself.

5.3 Choose one of these.
- When a 6-sided dice is thrown, what is the probability of throwing a 6 in six or fewer throws?
- Look at the total number of goals scored in the Premier division over the last few weeks. Use these figures to predict the total for next week.
  How close were you?
- Make a 6-sided dice by numbering the faces of a match box.
  Find the experimental probability of throwing a 1, 2, 3, ...

8 Drawing and measuring

8.1 Using only a ruler and compasses make accurate copies of these.

(a)

(b)

(c)

(d)

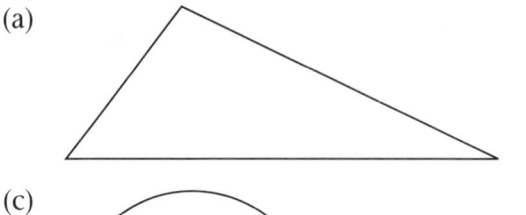

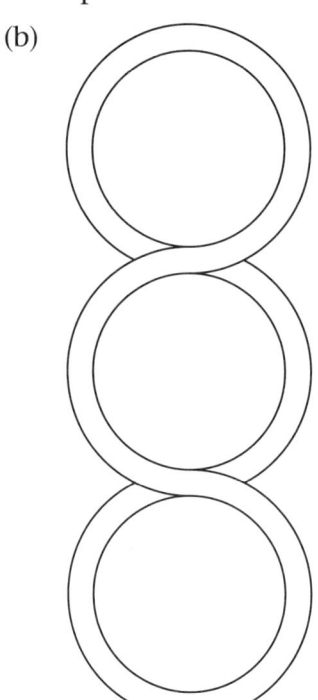

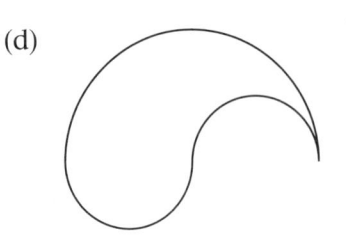

8.2 Construct these shapes.
You can use only a ruler and compasses.
(You may find it helpful to make a rough sketch of the shape first.)

(a) A triangle ABC, with ∠BAC = 30°, AB = 6 cm, AC = 8 cm.
Measure the length BC and ∠ABC.

(b) A triangle PQR, with ∠QPR = 40°, QR = 8 cm, RP = 7 cm.
Measure the side PQ and ∠PRQ.

(c) A triangle LMN with ∠MLN = 45°, LM = 5 cm and LN = 10 cm.
Measure the side MN and ∠LMN.

8.3 (a) The quadrilateral ABCD has AB = 6 cm, BC = 9 cm, CD = 8 cm, DA = 7 cm and BD = 4 cm. Construct the quadrilateral and measure the angles BAD, ADB and BCD.

(b) Is it possible to construct a quadrilateral if you only know the lengths of the four sides?

(c) Construct the pentagon ABCDE with BC = 6 cm, CD = 7 cm, DE = 5 cm, AE = 5 cm, ∠AED = 90°, ∠EDC = 120° and ∠DCB = 90°. Measure EB and BD.

9 Solving equations

9.1 Equations can be solved to give another equation or formula.
For example, take the equation

$x + m = n$

$x = n - m$ (subtracting m from each side).

The expression above gives x **in terms of** m and n.

Similarly x in terms of a and b in $ax = b$ is $x = \frac{b}{a}$.

Find x, in terms of any other letters used, in each of the following.

(a) $x - m = n$ (b) $kx = l$ (c) $rx - s = 0$

(d) $2x - p = q$ (e) $px + q = r$ (f) $px + q = r + s$

9.2 A general formula for a simple equation is

$$ax + b = cx + d$$

(In $6x + 3 = x + 13$, $a = 6$, $b = 3$, $c = 1$ and $d = 13$.)

Use algebra (and show all your working) to decide which of these is the correct formula for x.

$x = \frac{d-b}{a-c}$ $x = \frac{c-d}{a-b}$ $x = \frac{c-d}{b-a}$ $x = \frac{d-c}{b-a}$ $x = \frac{a-b}{c-d}$ $x = \frac{b-a}{c-d}$ $x = \frac{b-a}{d-c}$

10 Solving problems with algebra

10.1 (a) Here are the algebra steps involved in an 'I think of a number' trick.
Write the words which go with the trick. Try it on some friends or family.
What does the trick 'do'?

Instructions in words	Algebraic expressions
Think of any number	Let x be any number
...	$x + 15$
...	$3(x + 15) = 3x + 45$
...	$3x + 36$
...	$x + 12$
...	$x + 1$

(b) Repeat part (a) with these algebraic expressions.

Instructions in words	Algebraic expressions
Think of any number	Let x be any number
...	$2x$
...	$2x + 8$
...	$2x + 4$
...	4

10.2 (a) Use algebra to solve these 'age problems'.
Don't forget to check your answers using the original problem.

i) My age is the difference between my age in 4 years time and my age 4 years ago. How old am I now?

ii) The sum of the ages of Debbi, Tara and Jade is 34.
Debbi is 3 years older than Jade and Tara is 5 years younger than Jade.
How old is Debbi?

iii) The sum of Amy's age and Bob's age is 40. The sum of Bob's age and Clare's age is 34. The sum of Amy's and Clare's ages is 42.
How old is Bob?

(b) Make up and test some 'age problems' for yourself.
You could perhaps use names and ages of people in your family and base the puzzles on these.

10.3 Use algebra to solve these problems.

(a) The first number is four more than twice the second number.
The sum of the two numbers is 97. Find the two numbers.

(b) Andy has three times as many CDs as Beryl. Beryl has a quarter as many as Carole, who has four.
How many CDs does Derek have if he has two more than Andy?

(c) Make up some similar problems for yourself and try them on friends.

11 Inequalities

11.1 'I think of a number' problems can be used to **generate** inequalities.
Here is an example.

'English'	'Algebra'
I think of a number	x
add four to the number.	$x + 4$
The result is less than 12.	$x + 4 < 12$

As $x + 4 < 12$, so we can work out that $x < 8$ (the number is less than 8).
Write down and solve these two inequalities.

(a) I think of a number,
double it,
add four.
The result is greater than 20.

(b) I think of a number,
multiply it by 3,
subtract 10.
The result is less than 20.

(c) By some strange coincidence I thought of the same whole number both times! What number was it?

Invent some more puzzles like these.

Test them on your friends.

11.2 Here is an example of a number line graph showing the inequality $x \geq 2$.

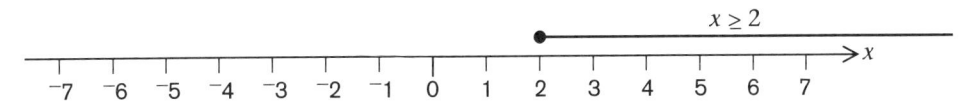

When the inequality is reflected in $x = 0$, the result is:

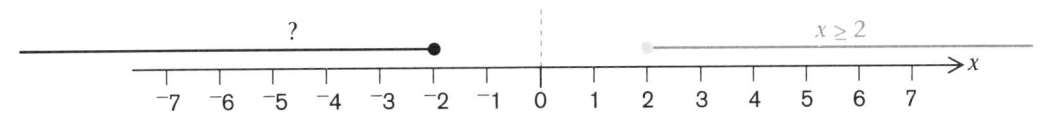

(a) Write down the inequality, ?, describing the reflected line.

(b) Investigate the effects of reflecting other inequalities in $x = 0$.
Be adventurous and try inequalities like $^-1 \leq x < 3$!
Jot down anything useful which you find.

11.3 (a) A straight line joining two points on a circle is called a **chord**.
Here are four chords.

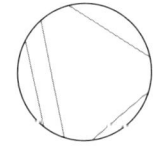

Write down an inequality involving the length (L) of a chord in a circle and the radius (R) of the circle.

(b) Here are two rectangles.
The perimeter of rectangle A is less than the perimeter of rectangle B.

Write the possible values of x, where x is a whole number.
(All lengths are in the same units.)

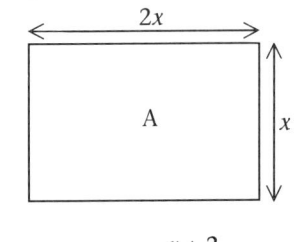

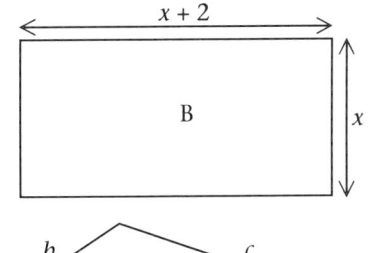

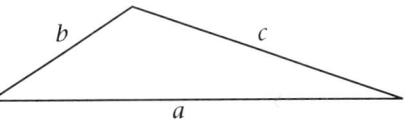

> **Challenge** Write down an inequality involving the longest side of a triangle, a, and the other two sides, b and c.

11.4 Pat wants to make up an inequality activity.
It involves finding whole numbers which fit:

$$^-2 \;\square\; ✗ \;\square\; 2$$

For example, $^-2 \;\boxed{\leq}\; ✗ \;\boxed{<}\; 2$

Are there solutions for all the possible combinations of <, ≤, > and ≥ put in the boxes? Investigate, perhaps make up a similar, better, game yourself.

12 Decimal practice

12.1 Make a collection of the nutritional information given on breakfast cereal packets. Use this information to draw up a table similar to the one in question C2 on page 40. Use consistent units so that you can compare the amount of various vitamins in the cereals.

12.2 This is a 4 by 4 magic square *but* four of the numbers are incorrect.

How long does it take you to find out which these are?

See how quickly a friend can find them. Are they faster than you?

Make up and test some similar 'speed' puzzles of your own.

0.1	0.15	0.05	0.04
0.08	0.02	0.11	0.14
0.03	0.06	0.16	0.07
0.13	0.12	0.01	0.09

12.3 A common mistake by students is to use a calculator, without thinking, in time calculations. For example, the length of time between 4.20 p.m. and 3.15 p.m. is 1 hour 5 minutes. By luck this just happens to be the answer to the decimal calculation 4.20 – 3.15. For many other calculations you won't be so lucky. The time between 3.20 and 4.15 is 55 minutes not 95 minutes – the answer you will get if you use a calculator without thinking! Investigate cases where a calculator gives the correct answer by pure chance and when it does not.

12.4 By adding decimal points and using as many zeros as you wish, make these calculations 'true'. There is more than one correct answer – just give one. The first one has been done for you.

(a) 12 + 8 = 2 ⟶ 1.2 + 0.8 = 2

(b) 11 – 99 = 11

(c) 799 + 201 = 1

(d) 998 + 2 = 1

(e) 2 – 19 = 1

Make up and try some similar puzzles on some friends.

13 Multiplication with decimals

13.1 Using only the digits 1, 2, 3, 4 and 5 once each and using just two decimal points, find a multiplication whose answer is 33.5.

Hint Before writing down any calculations look at the 'answer' to see if you can narrow down your choices.

Make up some similar puzzles. But before trying them out make sure that you test them yourself, by thinking through how someone else could logically solve them – without guessing!

13.2 Here are some multipliers to change metric measurements into Imperial ones.

To change	into	multiply by
centimetres	inches	0.4
metres	feet	3.3
kilometres	miles	0.6
grams	ounces	0.035
kilograms	pounds	2.2
tonnes	tons	0.98
litres	pints	1.8
litres	gallons	0.22

Use only the table and pencil and paper to change these metric measurements into the Imperial measurements given here.

(a) 30 cm into inches (30 cm is the length of a 'long' ruler).

(b) It is 340 km from London to York. How many miles is this?

(c) The tallest radio mast is in North Dakota, USA. It is 630 metres high. How many feet is this?

(d) One of the deepest holes drilled into the earth's surface is in Russia. It is 15 kilometres deep. What is this in miles?

(e) The heaviest load carried, in the UK, by road was a 79 m long bridge! It weighed just over 2 000 tonnes. What was this in tons?

Find some other records and change them into Imperial units *or* measure some items round your house or school and change these measurements into Imperial units.

14 Division with decimals

14.1 (a) Upper Primary pupils often use remainders when doing divisions.
For example, 461 ÷ 4 = 115 remainder 1
46 ÷ 5 = 9 remainder 1
57 ÷ 8 = 7 remainder 1.
Write down a few divisions which result in a remainder of 1.

(b) The answers to the divisions above, using decimals, are
461 ÷ 4 = 115.25
46 ÷ 5 = 9.2
57 ÷ 8 = 7.125
What is the connection between the remainder and the decimal part of the answer? Try not to use a calculator, but if you really need to …

(c) Can you find an easy way to calculate the remainder using just the decimal part of the answer?

14.2 Here are some division calculations and their answers.
Find the missing digits. There are two * in each puzzle.

(a) 0.99* ÷ 0.8 = 1.*4   (b) 66.12 ÷ *.2 = 5*.1

Show these to a friend and ask them to set you a 3* problem – can you solve it?

14.3 Investigate the truth (or otherwise) of each of these statements.

(a) Division by 0.9 is the same as multiplication by 1.1.
(b) "   "   " 0.6 " "   "   "   "   " 1.6
(c) "   "   " 0.5 " "   "   "   "   " 2.0
(d) "   "   " 0.4 " "   "   "   "   " 2.5
(e) "   "   " 0.2 " "   "   "   "   " 5.0
(f) "   "   " 0.08 " "   "   "   "   " 12.5

Illustrate your answers with examples.

Word list and definitions

Acute	An angle which is less than a right angle (90°).
Arrow head	A quadrilateral which has one inside angle greater than 180° and one line of symmetry.

line of symmetry

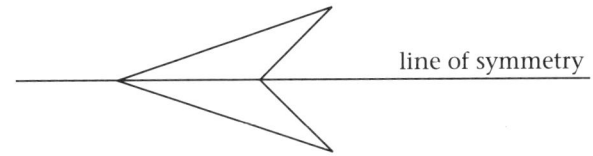

Bisect	When something such as a line or an angle is cut into two equal parts, we say that it is bisected.
Circumference	The distance going exactly once around the edge of a circle. This is the special name for the perimeter of a circle.
Congruent	Objects which are identical in shape and size are congruent.
Consecutive	Consecutive means following on in order. For example, 7, 8 and 9 are consecutive whole numbers and 11, 13 and 17 are consecutive prime numbers.
Difference	The difference of two numbers is the answer when the smaller number is subtracted from the larger number. For example, the difference between 3 and 7 is 4 (= 7 − 3).
Digit	Any single figure used to represent a number. In our number system there are ten digits, 0, 1, 2, 3, 4, 5, 6, 7, 8, and 9. The digits used in the number 12276 are 1, 2, 7 and 6.
Divisibility	If a number divided by another gives no remainder, the first number is divisible by the second number. For example, 16 ÷ 2 = 8, so 16 is divisible by 2.
Equation	A mathematical statement which says that two expressions are equal is called an equation. For example, the expression '2x + 6' and 'x + 15' can be made equal in the equation $2x + 6 = x + 15$.
Equivalent fraction	Fractions which have the same value are called equivalent fractions. For example, these fractions are equivalent: $\frac{4}{9}, \frac{8}{18}, \frac{12}{27}, \frac{20}{45}, \frac{40}{90}$
Estimate	Using a method to judge the value of a measurement or calculation. It is not the same as a guess.
Expression	A collection of numbers, symbols and letters with no linking symbol such as '=' or '>' is called an expression. These are all expressions: $2x^2 + 6$, x^2, $6 + 16$ and $x + x + 2y$.
Factor	The factors of a number are those numbers which divide exactly into the number. The factors of 30 are 1, 2, 3, 5, 6, 10, 15 and 30.
Frequency	The number of times an event or quantity occurs is the frequency of that event or quantity. The frequency of *x*s here is 4: ✗ ✗ ○ ○ ○ ○ ✗ ○ ✗. The **relative frequency** of ✗s is $\frac{4}{9}$.
Inequality	When a mathematical statement about the relative sizes of two expressions is made, the result is called an inequality. Some inequalities made from the expression '$x + 7$' and the expression '5' are $x + 7 \geq 5$, $x + 7 < 5$ and $x + 7 > 5$.
Mean	Gives an average/typical value for a set of data. To calculate it, total the data and divide this by the number of items.
Median	The middle value when a list of data is arranged in order of size. The median value of 6, 1, 7, 10 is 6.5, i.e. (6+7) ÷ 2.

Mode	The most frequent value. The modal value of 1, 2, 4, 4, 4, 5, 5, 6, 6, 7 is 4 because 4 occurs three times.
Multiple	A number which you get from another number by multiplication. For example, 77 (7 × 11) is a multiple of 7 and 11.
Obtuse	An obtuse angle is an angle greater than 90° and less than 180°.
Origin	The origin on a graph is the point with coordinates (0, 0).
Prime number	A number that has only two factors, itself and 1. For example, 7 = 7 × 1 – it cannot be written as the product of any other counting numbers. 1 is not a prime number – it has only one factor, which is 1.
Product	The product of a set of numbers is the result of multiplying them all together. The product of 4 and 6 is 4 × 6 = 24, the product of 4, 7 and 3 is 4 × 7 × 3 = 84.
Property	A property of an object is something which describes that object. For example, two of the properties of a square are that all its angles are the same and that all its sides are the same.
Range	The difference between the largest and smallest in a set of data. The range of 1, 5, 8, 19, 30, 31, 43 is (43 − 1) which is 42.
Recurring decimal	A decimal in which one or more digits are repeated 'for ever' is called a recurring decimal. For example, these divisions all result in recurring decimals, 1 ÷ 3, 1 ÷ 9, 20 ÷ 7.
Simplify	Simplify means to write in a shorter form. For example, $2x + x + x + 6y - y + 2y$ simplified is $4x + 7y$.
Square number	The result of multiplying a whole number by itself. Square numbers can be shown as a pattern of dots in the shape of a square. 1, 4, 9, 16, 25, 36, 49, and so on are all square numbers. 1 = 1 × 1 4 = 2 × 2 9 = 3 × 3
Substituting	When a letter in an expression is replaced by a number, we say that the number has been substituted for that letter. For example, the expression $2x + 4$ takes the value of 24 when 10 is substituted for x.
Sum	The sum of a set of numbers is another word for their total. For example, the sum of 2 and 7 is 9 (= 2 + 7), the sum of 4, 5 and 9 is 18.
Term	A number which is part of a number sequence is called a term of that sequence. In the sequence 3, 6, 15, 18, 21 ..., 3 is the first term, 6 the second term, and so on.

Triangle number	A number that can be shown as a pattern of dots in the shape of a triangle. 1, 3, 6, 10, 15, 21, 28, ... are all triangle numbers. The difference between terms increases by 1 each time (3 − 1 = 2, 6 − 3 = 3, 10 − 6 = 4, 15 − 10 = 5, and so on).
	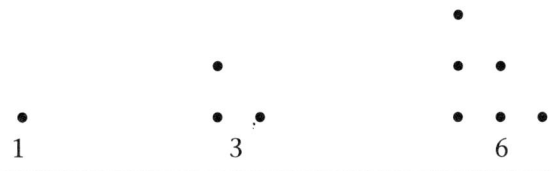 1 3 6
Vertex	The mathematical word for the corner of a shape (or solid). It is a point where sides (or edges) meet. These dots show vertices.
x-, y-coordinate	A point on a graph can be fixed by two numbers. These two numbers give its position with reference to the *x*- and *y*-axis, in the form (*x*-coordinate, *y*-coordinate).
	this point has coordinates (9, 4) (0, 0) the origin

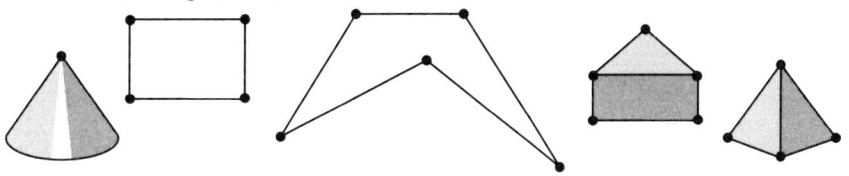

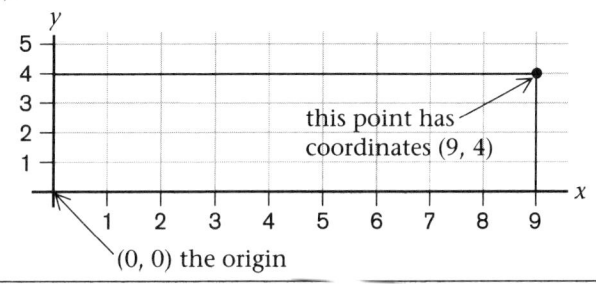